UNLEASHING KINGDOM AUTHORITY

FROM CONSUMER TO DISTRIBUTOR

DAVID S. PHILEMON

Royal Diadem Publishing Inc.

Dedication

To the Almighty God, my Rock, Refuge, and Source of all wisdom and strength. Thank You for Your unwavering love, grace, and the purpose You've placed within me. May this book bring glory to Your name and draw others closer to You.

And to my beloved spiritual parents, Dr. Paul and Dr. Mrs. Becky Paul Enenche, who have faithfully nurtured and guided me in this journey. Your example of unwavering devotion, godly counsel, and compassionate care has been a beacon of light and strength in my life. Thank you for standing as pillars of faith and for your steadfast commitment to the Kingdom.

ACKNOWLEDGMENTS

This book would not have been possible without the unwavering support, dedication, and talent of an extraordinary team. My deepest gratitude goes to each of you for your contributions, insights, and encouragement throughout this journey.

First and foremost, thank you to Rev. Mimi Philemon my dear wife, Rev. Shina Gentry, and and my assistant pastor Rev. Bright Amudoaghan for your incredible effort, encouragement, and belief in this project. Your support has been instrumental in bringing this vision to life.

To the dedicated leaders of Royal Diadem Publishing, Ide Imogie and Kishawna Bailey, I am immensely grateful for your belief in this project from the very beginning and for investing your time and energy into its development. Your creativity, dedication, and expertise have been the backbone of this endeavor.

I am especially grateful to the Royal Diadem Publishing team— Beulah Orogun, Emmanuella Ben-Eboh, Doyinsade Awodele, Kim Matthews, and Shante Gill, for your meticulous attention to detail, refining every page and ensuring that each word reflects our vision.

A heartfelt thank you to my family, friends, and colleagues whose unwavering support and belief in this project gave me the courage and strength to see it through.

Finally, thank you to all the readers and supporters who make this work meaningful. I am humbled and honored to share this journey with each of you.

With all my gratitude,
David Philemon

CONTENTS

INTRODUCTION

In the days we live in, we are witnessing a divine shift. God is no longer focused on merely blessing us with the benefits of the Kingdom; instead, He is looking for those who will serve as conduits of His grace, power, and glory. The time for hoarding blessings has passed. God is in a hurry to distribute Kingdom benefits to those He knows are prepared to be channels of His glory, those who will not just receive but release, not just be filled but overflow into the lives of others. He is actively searching for Kingdom distributors—people who will take what they receive from Him and share it, impacting lives, communities, and nations.

Sadly, the **consumer mentality** has infiltrated the Church. Too often, believers approach their faith with a mindset of "what can I get?" rather than "what can I give?" This mentality has dulled our spiritual edge, eroding the grace and glory that God intended for His people to carry. We have become content with receiving but hesitant to give. We have become accustomed to being the recipients of God's blessings but hesitant to assume the role of distributors.

But God is calling us higher. He is issuing a clarion call to His people, urging us to rise above the consumer mindset and step into our true Kingdom identity. He is calling us to be contributors, dispensers, and distributors of His power, not merely consumers. The days of spiritual passivity are over. The days of Kingdom action are here.

The Kingdom of God was never meant to be consumed in isolation—it was meant to be shared, spread, and multiplied.

As Kingdom distributors, we are entrusted with carrying God's presence into the world, embodying His love, and releasing His resources into every sphere of influence.

This book is a blueprint for the believer who is ready to make the shift, who is ready to transition from merely receiving to actively distributing. You will discover how to walk in **Kingdom authority** and how to partner with God in the divine mandate of bringing Heaven to Earth. You will learn how to become a vessel through which the blessings of God flow into your family, community, and the world at large.

The question is no longer, "What can I receive?" but "How can I distribute what God has given me?" God is looking for you to rise to the occasion. He is ready to release His unlimited resources to those who understand that they are blessed to be a blessing. This is your invitation to step into your divine role as a **Kingdom distributor**, shifting from consumption to contribution, from receiving to releasing. The time is now, and the call is urgent. Will you answer?

CHAPTER 1

THE CALL TO BE A DISTRIBUTOR, NOT A CONSUMER

"Freely you have received the kingdom's power, so freely release it to others."

– Matthew 10:8 (TPT)

The world we live in today is centered around one thing: consumption. From social media to fast food, consumerism has become the driving force of society. Yet, God's economy operates by a completely different standard. In the Kingdom of God, the more you give, the more you are positioned to receive. And in this hour, God is no longer looking for consumers. He is actively searching for distributors—those who will not hoard His blessings, but freely give what they have received. This is the call to step out of a mindset that says, "What can I get?" and into a life that declares, "How can I give?"

In this chapter, we will explore how shifting from being a consumer to a distributor positions you to live in the overflow of God's blessings and authority. The journey from consumer to distributor is not just a shift in mindset but a transformation in identity, one that allows you to fully unleash Kingdom authority and become a vessel through which God's ultimate power flows.

THE KINGDOM PRINCIPLE: FREELY GIVE, FREELY RECEIVE

Jesus' mandate in *Matthew 10:8* is clear—what we have freely received from God, we are called to give away freely. But how often do we, even as believers, find ourselves holding onto the blessings and favor God has given us out of fear or greed? This consumer mentality subtly creeps in, creating a blockage in our spiritual lives. We become like a reservoir that has stopped flowing.

Imagine a reservoir built to supply water to an entire city. As long as it flows, life is sustained. But what happens if that reservoir stops distributing water? It stagnates. It becomes contaminated, unable to serve its purpose. Likewise, as believers, we are designed to receive and distribute God's grace, favor, and power. The moment we stop distributing —whether it is through love, generosity, or service—we risk becoming spiritually stagnant.

A consumer generation will always be a frustrated generation. Unfortunately, everyone has become a consumer. The consumer mentality has eroded grace and glory, especially from the Body of Christ. God is not seeking or looking for consumers and neither is our world. Instead of being a consumer, become a contributor.

CONSUMER CULTURE VERSUS KINGDOM CULTURE

We are surrounded with consumer culture that goes much beyond mere physical goods. It shapes all elements of our lives, including our relationships and even our faith. We have been taught to ask all the time, "What's in it for me?" or "How does this benefit me personally?" By means of a clandestine infiltration, this self-centered mindset has entered the church and transformed a sizable portion of the members into spiritual consumers.

Sometimes when we pray to God, we arrive to him carrying a large list of requests: "Lord, bless me." Give me something, Lord. Lord, I do indeed need." While asking God for help is not necessarily sinful, the problem arises when our interaction with Him is limited rather than the relationship itself. We run the danger of becoming spiritual parasites when we live our lives purely for our own benefit instead of matching ourselves with God's greater mission. Conversely, the kingdom's culture is predicated on the ideas of distribution and participation. Jesus arrived to serve not only but also to be served.

Our perfect model is him. All those who follow Him, he expects, will have the same selflessness. Jesus challenges His disciples in John 13:14 (TPT)

"Follow the example that I've set for you and wash one another's dirty feet. Treat one another the same way I have just taken care of you."

This great remark captures the way the Kingdom lives: one receives benefits from God and then shares those gifts with others. God's main goal is not to only grant to you all the benefits His realm has to provide. Instead, He wants you to become a conduit through which other people could receive those advantages.

This change from consumer to distributor helps us to line up with God's heart and intent. This is a big change that affects our own spiritual growth as well as positions us to be agents of God's love and power in the environment we live in. Adopting this Kingdom perspective helps us to enter the fullness of our calling as believers and engage actively in the scheme God has to bless and change the planet.

THE RESERVOIR OF GRACE: WHAT FLOWS IN, MUST FLOW OUT

God has positioned each of us as a reservoir, designed to be continually filled with His grace, wisdom, and power. But that reservoir must flow out to others. The more you pour out, the more God pours in. This is a foundational principle of Kingdom living.

Consider the Dead Sea, a body of water that has no outlets. It receives fresh water from the Jordan River but does not distribute it. As a result, it has become one of the saltiest bodies of water on earth, where nothing can grow or live. Compare that to the Sea of Galilee, which receives water and flows it out into the Jordan River. It is teeming with life, providing sustenance for the region. This is the stark contrast between a life that hoards God's blessings and a life that freely distributes what God has given.

One major scriptural principle is that you never run out of that which you are a giver of, including pain and headache. You will never run out of grace and glory if you are a distributor of grace and glory.

THE GENEROSITY OF R.G. LETOURNEAU

Let me share a real-life example of R.G. LeTourneau, a businessman and devout Christian who understood this principle. In the 1930s, LeTourneau made a commitment to God to give 90% of his income and live on just 10%. People

thought he was crazy, but he believed in the principle of distributing what he had received. As he poured out, God continued to bless his business beyond what he could have imagined. By the time he died, LeTourneau was known as the "God's businessman," using his wealth to further the Gospel and support countless Christian endeavors. He understood that he was not just a consumer of God's blessings but a distributor of them.

KINGDOM AUTHORITY UNLEASHED THROUGH GIVING

Then Jesus came close to them and said,
"All authority of the universe has been given to

me." – Matthew 28:18 TPT

God hands you plenty—more grace, more power, more authority—when you accept the responsibility of a distributor. This is not because you have earned it by your own merits but rather because you have shown that you are not a fixed reservoir gathering His benefits. Rather, you have turned into a free flowing channel spreading what He provides. This power reflects the heart of God Himself since it is firmly based in humility and service rather than in self-promotion or selfish benefit.

Think of the life of Jesus, our model perfect. Though His life was defined by continual giving and unselfish distribution, He wielded all authority in heaven and on earth (Matthew 28:18). From healing the ill to raising the dead, feeding the multitudes to instructing the masses, Jesus never stopped pouring out. For those around Him, his existence was an ongoing stream of divine love and strength. He walked in an unequalled degree of kingdom power exactly because He was the ultimate distributor.

We open another level of spiritual power when we change our emphasis from consuming to giving. This ability enables us to offer worldly issues Kingdom answers. We become conduits of God's power, able to speak life into lifeless circumstances, give hope to the despairing, and show the truth of God's kingdom in observable terms. Moreover, this distributor attitude helps us to see rewards and spiritual talents from another angle.

Rather than considering them as personal trophies or successes, we regard them as means of advancing the Kingdom. Every gift, every favor, and every discovery presents chances to bless others and increase God's impact. This change helps us to experience even more powerful movements of God's Spirit in and through our lives and more precisely connects us with His heart. God wants us to be conduits of His gifts to others, and we can get closer to His desire when we change our focus from accumulation to distribution. With this attitude, we can be open channels through which His grace and love might wash over people, changing their lives for the better. At the end of the day, adopting a distributor mindset allows us to change not just our own lives but also the lives of those around us.

SHIFTING FROM BLESSING SEEKERS TO
BLESSING CHANNELS

Simply seeking blessings and acting as a conduit for favors differ greatly. Consumers are always seeking the next miracle, invention, or blessing. But as we start distributing, we really begin to see that we are the breakthrough, the miracle, the benefit someone else is ferociously yearning for. This change of attitude is a basic metamorphosis of our identity, not only a change in behavior. We welcome the reality that each of us is privileged to bless others.

Abraham's promise from God in Genesis 12:2 (TPT) masterfully captures this idea:

> *"Follow me, and I will make you into a great nation.*
> *I will exceedingly bless and prosper you, and I will*
> *make you famous"*
> – Genesis 12:2 TPT

Keep in mind that God's favor wasn't supposed to stop with Abraham. It meant to pass through him blessing whole countries. God's abundance also flows most naturally to those ready to let it pass through them. When we realize we are conduits rather than only receivers, we enter a sphere of spiritual power affecting heaven as well as earth.

Our attitude to spiritual development and ministry is drastically changed by this distributor perspective. "How can

I be used by God to bless others?" we start to question instead of "What can I get from God?" This change of viewpoint lets God's power show itself in and through our lives in fresh directions. We grow more sensitive to the guidance of the Holy Spirit, more aware of the needs surrounding us, and more ready to walk forth in faith to be the response to another's prayer. Moreover, assuming the responsibility of a distributor helps us to match God's heart for expansion and giving.

When we offer what looks small in our hands freely, God can double it for His glory, just as Jesus took five loaves and two fish and multiplied them to feed thousands. This idea holds true for all elements of our life, including our time, abilities, knowledge, and spiritual gifts, not only for material blessings. We place ourselves to experience even more great degrees of God's supply and strength as we freely offer what we have received.

THE BLESSING OF OVERFLOW

As you embrace the call to be a distributor, God promises that your life will be marked by overflow. In *Luke 6:38*, Jesus says,

> *"Give generously and generous gifts will be given back to you, shaken down to make room for more. Abundant gifts will pour out upon you with such an overflowing measure that it will run over the top! Your measurement of generosity becomes the measurement of your return."*
> – Luke 6:38 (TPT)

This chapter vividly depicts God's economy: the more you contribute, the more you set yourself to be in demand. This receiving, however, is for giving once again, therefore generating a lovely circle of blessings and distribution rather than for stockpiling. This invitation to be a distributor asks us to reconsider our attitude to life, faith, and the Kingdom of God profoundly. It's about turning our viewpoint from a self-centered "What can I get?" to a kingdom-minded "What can I give?" This change is about matching our hearts with God's giving nature, not only about deeds.

Along with gaining more Kingdom authority, we become essential tools in God's big scheme to bring His grace, power, and glory to a planet sorely in need. God is aggressively looking for those who would be His power distributors. He is seeking vessels ready to carry His anointing, not for their own benefit but for the good of others. Our resolve to be vessels of His blessings determines this heavenly search, not our performance or perfection.

Now the question is: Are you prepared to respond to this call? Adopting the distributive perspective also calls for great confidence in God's provision. It requires standing out in faith and occasionally giving when our natural thinking makes no sense. But as we freely give and trust God, we sometimes find He offers in ways we never would have thought possible. Not only in our lives but also in the lives of people around us, this faith creates the path for miracles. Becoming distributors helps us to participate in God's fantastic economy in which five loaves and two fish can feed thousands, where little becomes much under the hands of a loving God.

CHAPTER 2

THE POWER OF CONSECRATION AND ALIGNMENT

"To surrender yourselves to God to be his sacred, living sacrifices. And live in holiness, experiencing all that delights his heart."

– Romans 12:1 (TPT)

The journey from consumer to distributor begins with a single, yet profound step—consecration. God does not just anoint anyone; He anoints those who have set themselves apart for His use. Consecration is the process of dedicating yourself fully to God's purpose, a deliberate act of surrender that realigns your heart, desires, and actions with His will. This alignment with God's purpose is essential for becoming a distributor of His resources, blessings, and power. Without it, we risk becoming vessels that are clogged, preventing the flow of God's grace through us.

In this chapter, we will explore how the power of consecration and alignment sets you apart for the highest calling in God's Kingdom—becoming a channel through which His blessings flow to the world.

WHAT IS CONSECRATION?

Consecration is a deep idea; consecration transcends simple outward expressions of devotion. This transforming process involves the whole offering of our mind, body, and spirit as a live sacrifice to God, therefore touching the very heart of our being. Romans 12:1 (TPT) instructs us to *"offer your bodies as a living sacrifice, holy and pleasing to God—this is your true and proper worship."* Consecration is not a one-time event but a lifestyle of constant surrender and alignment to God's will.

This is a way of life of ongoing submission and alignment with God's will, not a one-time occurrence or a surface ritual. To really understand consecration, picture a conduit delivering fresh water to a residence. Should this pipe be contaminated or blocked, it cannot effectively move the water it is designed to carry. Likewise, we become useless conduits for God's benefit if our life is crowded with sinfulness, distractions, or worldly goals.

Then consecration is the process of cleaning and clearing that conduit, thereby enabling the unfettered flow of God's anointing across us without constraint. Often on our spiritual path, we look for the fastest way to get to our goals. Still, the spiritual route is usually the fastest and most straight-forward one. God wants us to grow to be able to get His straight replies. He yearns for us to have the spiritual acuity to recognize His voice and get His direction right away.

"I will answer them before they even call to me.
While they are still talking to me about their needs,
I will answer their prayers!"
                              – Isaiah 65:24 TLB

Being empowered by the same Spirit who raised Christ from the grave makes this immediacy in divine response more than just a benefit of being a Christian.

We have to match ourselves with the Spirit of God, the

source of all power, if we are to experience this degree of spiritual efficacy. Still, individuals who approach spiritual concerns lightly should not expect spiritual gains. Many Christians find it difficult to properly bear God's power when they are too preoccupied with earthly issues. Although the spirit realm is sometimes seen as complicated and enigmatic, mastery of some basic ideas helps us to reach it. Often more clearly than abstract ideas are personal experiences that show these spiritual truths.

I remember a morning when I was pretty hungry and ready to eat, but the Holy Spirit told me to fast for a particular goal. Though I was physically hungry, I decided to follow this heavenly direction. Although at first glance, aligning with God's will seems easy, it often entails fierce spiritual struggle. I have made it a top goal never to disobey spiritual laws, notably the commandment of identifying with my spiritual father, Pastor Dr. Paul Enenche, and my spiritual lineage. Though I know I cannot afford to stray from the oil and impartation that emanates from my spiritual background, this dedication comes at a significant cost and calls for great sacrifice.

In the spiritual sphere, impartation is the supernatural bestowal of access and power, usually to people who would seem unsuited by human criteria. The spirit realm is quite conscious of our lack of qualifications or otherwise. The narrative of Gehazi, Elisha's servant, as told in 2 Kings 4:29–31 (TLB), deftly illustrates this spiritual reality

> "Then he said to Gehazi, "Quick, take my staff! Don't talk to anyone along the way. Hurry! Lay the staff upon the child's face." But the boy's mother said, "I swear to God that I won't go home without you." So Elisha returned with her. Gehazi went on ahead and laid the staff upon the child's face, but nothing happened. There was no sign of life. He returned to meet Elisha and told him, "The child is

still dead."

– 2 Kings 4:29-31 TLB

his story offers deep spiritual understanding of the results of a heart that has started to stray from its divine calling. Gehazi's inability to raise the child with Elisha's staff revealed a deeper spiritual detachment than just a matter of wrong technique. Gehazi had let his mind drift from the purity and dedication needed to operate in God's might, even as he was accompanying a great prophet.

Elisha gave Gehazi precise, unambiguous directions: act quickly, stay away from distractions, and place the staff on the child's face. A sign of spiritual authority, the staff could help to direct God's power. Gehazi was useless nonetheless because of his inner condition. His mind had already started to wander, a spiritual declension that would eventually show up as his avarice for riches and status, as the narrative of Naaman in 2 Kings 5 would show.

This spiritual wander produced a barrier in the divine force flow. Gehazi lacked the fundamental internal qualities, purity of heart, and single-minded focus required to enable a miracle while possessing all the exterior elements: the tools, the position, and proximity to the man of God. This produced a clear spiritual collapse: "nothing happened." Elisha stayed quite close to God, on the other hand. Discerning this spiritual truth, the boy's mother insisted that Elisha personally visit to see her son restored.

She understood that the guy whose spirit was exactly in line with God possessed actual authority, not in any physical item or assigned choreography. Gehazi's hands failing the rod expose a fundamental spiritual principle. His mind was far from concentrated, even if he might not have had physical conversations during his trip. His lack of spiritual alignment and mental diversion made him unable to carry God's ability to produce instantaneous outcomes.

This reminds us poignantly that some people find

it difficult to show God's power since they cannot keep spiritual focus and alignment. Maintaining and reaching this degree of spiritual effectiveness comes with a great price. One must constantly invest and give up something to be able to see spiritual realities before others and to overcome difficult problems. This is a road of continuous devotion and coordination with God's will. We must recognize that just being near power or possessing spiritual symbols, like Elisha's staff, is inadequate.

In God's Kingdom, true effectiveness calls for a heart totally dedicated and in line with Him, free from distractions, personal goals, or stray ideas. Even our spiritual instruments and power might lose effectiveness when our minds stray from God. It's not only about external gestures or symbols; most importantly, our hearts' internal state counts. The degree of devotion needed for best spiritual performance is shockingly great.

Fundamentally, consecration at this level is a person's capacity to separate and disengage their ideas from usual human patterns of thinking.

Revelation 4:10 (TLB) clearly illustrates this idea:

> *"The twenty-four Elders fell down before him and worshiped him, the Eternal Living One, and cast their crowns before the throne,*
> *singing, "O Lord, you""*.
> – Revelation 4:10 TLB

Absolute consecration is the capacity to separate our success from ourselves.

Our crowns, such as our accomplishments, our standing, and our skills, are not really ours. Entitlement can drain us of effectiveness and spiritual strength. One needs deep respect and humility. One of the strongest weapons in the enemy's toolkit, worldliness helps to neutralize possible power bearers. Then consecration is the capacity to separate oneself from personal glory to become bearers of God's glory, therefore displaying His power and presence in the earth.

Given end-time prophecies, the value of consecration becomes even more apparent.

> *"The Holy Spirit has explicitly revealed: At the end of this age, many will depart from the true faith one after another, devoting themselves to spirits of deception and following demon-inspired revelations".*
>
> – 1 Timothy 4:1 TPT

Maintaining a consecrated life becomes not only helpful but also essential for spiritual survival and efficacy in these trying circumstances. Every Christian should grow to have a strong and fervent wish to be a front-liner in His kingdom, God says.

This is a wonderful and commendable ambition. But Satan frequently uses this great ambition as a weapon to divert and discredit people who first set out with good intentions. For example, some people who start their ministry with pure intentions may find themselves sidetracked as their influence increases by thinking about personal success and glory. Given these spiritual realities, consecration becomes clear as a non-negotiable need for anybody who wants to be strong in God's kingdom. In God's perspective, true brilliance is not about self-gratification or personal glory.

Rather, it's about voluntarily becoming a very useful and sanctified conduit for God's kingdom and human welfare. Overcoming spiritual resistance and removing obstacles in our way of effectiveness in God's work requires consecration as a potent key. It's a process of separating ourselves from God and committing everything of our lives to Him. This commitment helps us to get closer to God, therefore strengthening us for the spiritual conflicts we encounter and allowing us to resist the plans of the enemy.

The call to consecration is, ultimately, a summons to a more deliberate, deeper path with God. **It is a crucial non-negotiable requirement.** It forces us to look at our hearts, motives, and behaviors, therefore bringing every element of our life into line with God's will. By adopting this dedicated way of life, we set ourselves to be more efficient means of God's power and blessings in a world sorely in need of His touch. Recognizing that all we are and all we have belongs to Him, may we, like the twenty-four elders in Revelation, learn to place our crowns before the throne. By doing this, we allow more of His power and presence to flow through us, therefore acting as the sanctified vessels He can employ to transform our planet.

THE ROLE OF ALIGNMENT IN KINGDOM DISTRIBUTION

Combining the two great principles of alignment and consecration can radically transform a person's life and impact in God's kingdom. Aligning oneself with God's will increases the effectiveness of consecration, a wonderful first step towards personal spiritual development on its own. Let's look at these concepts more closely to find how they support a life influenced by the divine and well-lived.

Consecration is just putting one's life aside for God's use. It's the deliberate decision to devote one's time, money, and resources to a more significant cause. Just being ready for God to use this act of submission is quite impressive. Still, if one is not in correct alignment, the power of consecration may go wasted. Seen through the prism of spiritual development, being spiritually aligned means bringing one's life into line with God's plan and schedule. It's all about matching our will, actions, and decisions with God's ideal course of events for each of us.

This principle reminds me of fine-tuning an instrument. Like a well tuned instrument, the life that fits God's design vibrates with His divine harmony. Imagine a brilliant pianist playing a challenging piece on an out-of-tune piano. The outcome would be an awkward and dissonant performance regardless of the musician's degree of talent. In the same vein, leading a holy life out of harmony could make you feel disappointed and have less effect. If we deviate from His exact directions or timing, our efforts, even if we are dedicated and hard for God, may go flat.

Those who have mastered both alignment and consecration are the real Kingdom distributors. These people have not only set themselves apart for God's use but also aimed to discover and obey His will for their lifetime. Under the direction of the master musician, they are like beautifully tuned instruments ready to perform any song he requests.

Incorrect alignment of consecration can cause burnout and dissatisfaction. When we depend simply on our own knowledge and skills, even with the best of intentions, we run the danger of getting demoralized and exhausted. However, the mercy of God, which is available to those who follow His will, gives us the superhuman strength and clarity needed for success.

Though they are wonderful spiritual principles and habits, consecration and alignment are not confined to those who work full-time in ministry or are ordained into religious professions. Regardless of their line of work or background, these ideas apply to every believer everywhere. God wants His people used wherever, in the boardroom, the classroom, the hospital, even the house. Consider a businessman who answers God's direction and commits his firm to advancing

God's kingdom. Rather than only a financial firm, this entrepreneur sees their creation as a means of evangelizing and turning a profit. Their company strategy is predicated on God's principles rather than profit.

Above all, they respect integrity; they treat their staff and the community kindly; and they view their work as a means of serving others rather than as a means of personal benefit at all costs. This unity and commitment help the business to become a useful tool for Kingdom expansion. Through the power of God's love, the owner may not only experience financial success but also find many opportunities to influence employees, customers, and even rivals. Compassionate leadership and ethical business practices help to transform the workplace into a mission field where God's ideas are reflected and lives are impacted.

One excellent example of this is the well-known fast-food chain Chick-fil-A. S. Truett. Cathy achieved quite a remarkable thing when he opened his restaurant in Hapeville, Georgia, in 1946. He implemented what is still in effect today as a policy of closing Sundays for business. Cathy's desire to honor God and provide his workers and himself a day for prayer and recuperation drove this choice. Closing on one of the busiest days for fast-food sales could have impeded the company's expansion, as many business gurus would have expected. But the result has been absolutely opposite. With systemwide revenues exceeding $21.6 billion, which exceeded $18.8 billion in the previous year, reports from FranchiseTimes.com show Chick-fil-A reached a significant milestone in 2023.

Forecasts for business revenue in 2019 show it to be $12.6 billion, a stunning increase of about $10 billion from just five years ago. Chick-fil-A's remarkable years-long expansion has made the business a major force in the fast-food industry. The company's success may be mostly ascribed to its unwavering dedication to the ideas of alignment and consecration. Apart from its financial success, Chick-fil-A has gained recognition for its excellent customer service and friendly corporate culture, as they have committed their company strategies to respect God and match their activities with Biblical values.

This actual situation clearly illustrates the effectiveness of consecration and alignment in business. Thus, we can personally observe how God might bless us abundantly when we follow His will and live in line with His values.

> "What delight comes to the one who follows God's ways! His passion is to remain true to the Word of "I AM," meditating day and night on the true revelation of light. He will be standing firm like a flourishing tree planted by God's design, deeply rooted by the brooks of bliss, bearing fruit in every season of his life. He is never dry, never fainting, ever blessed, ever prosperous."
> – Psalm 1:1-3 TPT

This chapter graphically shows the advantages of leading a life committed to God and in line with His desire.

Like trees grown by streams of water, devotees of God's methods often find great resonance in His Word since they get firmly rooted and always fed. They are productive not only at one stage of life but throughout all. The blessings this chapter promises transcend simple financial gain. Since this life experiences God's favor in all respects, it is overflowing with blessings. This gift manifests as endurance in trying circumstances (never dry, never fainting), impact and growth (fruit in every season), monetary, emotional, and spiritual riches. When we commit and organize our complete life with God's will, we open ourselves to get His bountiful advantages.

The grace and power we are given will help us to overcome whatever challenges we find in our lives. At last, the best approach to changing God's kingdom is to be totally dedicated to His will and cooperate with Him. We have to be ready to separate ourselves for God's use and give our lives top attention so that they fit His will. Conforming our lives to these criteria opens the path for others to partake in God's love and power, as well as for ourselves to savor everything He has to give.

THE POWER OF SACRIFICE

One cannot speak of consecration without addressing the role of sacrifice. Every major figure in the Bible who walked in divine power did so through sacrifice. Take Abraham's willingness to offer Isaac as an example; this was not a trivial matter. God had promised Abraham that his descendants would come via Isaac, the son of promise. Abraham, however, had enough faith in God to offer that pledge on the cross.

This significant offering serves as an example of the degree of submission required for consecration. In a similar vein, Moses had to give up Egypt's comforts and his regal status in order to carry out God's plan. He rejected the transient delights of life in the palace in favor of empathizing with his people's misery. Another great act of consecration is Esther's risking her life to save her people. She didn't merely enter the king's presence with a plea; she fasted, prayed, and aligned herself with God's will, despite the possibility of death. In each case, God honored their sacrifices by using them mightily, not only for their personal gain but for the blessing and deliverance of many.

The key to accessing heavenly authority is sacrifice. It is a continual willingness to give go of one's own goals, comforts, and ambitions in favor of God's purpose rather than an isolated act. We're frequently asked to give up things we've held dear, like our time, our dreams, or even our relationships.

But God works most strongly during these times of surrender.

By sacrificing your desires in favor of what God wants, you open up a path for His power to pass through unhindered. This is an important positioning because it takes oneself out of the situation and opens the door for divine intervention. We make greater space for God to act through us the more we let go. This is a life totally given up and directed towards the goals of heaven; this is the essence of consecration. I'll give a stirring personal account of how consecration and alignment are crucial to releasing the power of the kingdom.

There was a season in my ministry when I felt the call to enter an extended period of fasting and prayer. It wasn't easy; separating myself from my peers and daily distractions felt like a loss at the time. But I knew it was necessary. I sensed a deep stirring in my spirit that God wanted to do something extraordinary, and the only way to access it was through consecration. I set myself apart, aligning my heart and spirit to hear God's voice clearly.

During that time, I began to experience miracles on a scale I had never imagined; people were healed, and spiritual breakthroughs occurred. It was as though my obedience had caused the sky to open. This was a direct result of my consecration, not something that came about as a result of my years of ministry or any particular gift. During that season, I exuded spiritual power without fail, and it all began with my resolve to fully align myself with God.

One particular story stands out. During that time of fasting and prayer, I felt a clear instruction from the Holy Spirit to organize a healing and deliverance service in a village known for its stronghold of demonic forces. The reputation of the village was intimidating; even the chief priests were said to be dangerous, with spiritual power that few dared to challenge. Despite advice from some who believed the timing was off or the assignment too risky, I trusted the instruction I had received.

My confidence wasn't in my ability but in the authority I had gained through consecration. The outcome was miraculous. Healing broke forth, bonds of oppression were destroyed, and before our own eyes, the same powers people dreaded were destroyed. During the spiritual conflict, even the chief priest, a strong man in that area, passed away; his casket traveled across the village as evidence of God's might. The stronghold over that land was broken, not by my strength but by the power of God moving through a consecrated vessel. This experience was a powerful reminder that consecration aligns us with God's authority in ways that go beyond our natural abilities.

Another powerful example of consecration and alignment is found in the life of Daniel. When Daniel was taken captive to Babylon, he made a bold decision that went against the norm. He consecrated himself by refusing to defile himself with the king's food and wine. The king's table was lavish, filled with delicacies that many would have eagerly partaken in, especially after being displaced from their homeland. But Daniel knew that consuming such food would violate the dietary laws given by God. He took a stand not out of rebellion but out of reverence for the covenant he had with God.

> *"However, Daniel determined in his heart not to contaminate himself with the food and wine from the royal table, so he begged the chief official to exempt him from the royal diet".*
> – Daniel 1:8 TPT

This act of consecration was also an act of alignment. Daniel was setting himself up for heavenly favor by deciding to respect God's laws even in a strange country. The outcomes were clear as well. God gave him not only official favor but also supernatural insight and understanding. Daniel, by supernatural revelation, answered King Nebuchadnezzar's frightening dreams that none of the magicians or wise men could understand, therefore saving many lives in the process. His commitment prepared him to influence the world, not to remove him from it.

Daniel's life shows that consecration is about still being useful in the world while yet matching with God's will. This is a lesson for all of us: our dedication to God will provide chances for His power to be shown even in surroundings that dishonor Him. Daniel prayed, not presenting a brief, halfhearted appeal. No, his prayer was passionate and his allegiance clear-cut. He fasted, humbled himself before God, and fervently kept seeking Him.

This was a way of life of consecration, not only a single act of loyalty. If we are to break through the spiritual barriers the enemy sets before us, we too must be willing to consecrate ourselves before God. This might mean fasting, extended prayer, or setting aside distractions to seek God's face. As James 4:8 reminds us, "Come near to God, and he will come near to you." Fasting and prayer are spiritual disciplines that position us to hear from God and receive the strength, insight, and angelic assistance needed to overcome obstacles in our path.

Jesus Christ is the perfect illustration of alignment and dedication. His life was the epitome of surrender and selflessness. As the lovely Romans 12:1 (TLB) states.

> "And so, dear brothers, I plead with you to give your bodies to God. Let them be a living sacrifice, holy— the kind he can accept. When you think of what he has done for you, is this too much to ask?"

Jesus lived a lifelong sacrifice in addition to offering Himself as a sacrifice on the cross.

Every choice He made and every deed He did from the start of His mission were in accordance with the Father's will. Jesus says in John 6:38,

"For I have come here from heaven to do the will of
God who sent me, not to have my own way".

When Jesus offered the ultimate sacrifice on the cross to save humanity, this alignment with the will of the Father reached its zenith.

The greatest miracle of all was made possible by His consecration: eternal life for everyone who would believe in Him. Jesus' example teaches us that true consecration is about laying down our lives, not just in moments of crisis but daily, as we seek to fulfill God's purpose. His life was the ultimate demonstration of what it means to be fully aligned with God, and through that alignment, He unleashed the full power of the kingdom on earth.

CONSECRATION UNLOCKS GREATER AUTHORITY

Being consecrated and in line not only helps you to share God's benefits but also imparts more spiritual authority. God does not hand Kingdom power to individuals who are not totally committed and in line with Him, much like a military general does not assign command to an undisciplined soldier. Understanding the mechanism of spiritual strength depends on this principle.

Authority follows automatically from a life dedicated to God's will; it cannot be earned by simply praying louder than others. This is the reason many find it difficult to work in the fullness of God's might. You might witness someone pray sincerely for healing, yet nothing comes of it. Though they use faith-filled language, they do not see the outcomes. Often, in these circumstances, consecration and alignment are the missing links. When we are consecrated—set apart for God's purposes—and in line with His will, authority flows without too much physical gymnastics or effort. Miracles, healing, and discoveries occur naturally from a life firmly anchored in God's will; they cannot be produced by simple effort.

God is urging His people to more alignment and devotion. He looks for people who will really set themselves apart and walk in line with His purposes, not only follow their beliefs. Saying you believe in God or engage in religious activities is insufficient; God wants deeper commitment. Your heart and mind will start to line up with His will, and you will see blessings start to pour naturally. The power you formerly battled to obtain is now here and active, enabling you to influence His kingdom more broadly.

To become a distributor in God's Kingdom, consecration and alignment are without a doubt the ultimate keys to moving from a consumer attitude. Concentrating oneself helps you to present yourself as a holy, ready tool for God's use. And by means of alignment, you open a route for His power, knowledge, and benefits. The question then is: Are you prepared to present yourself as a living sacrifice, totally in line with God's will? If so, get ready to be used as a Kingdom distributor in very remarkable ways. The journey starts with your readiness to let God's power pass through you.

CHAPTER 3

THE BATTLE FOR YOUR FAITH

"Fight on for God. Hold tightly to the eternal life that God has given you and that you have confessed with such a ringing confession before many witnesses."

– 1 Timothy 6:12 (TLB)

F aith is the currency of the Kingdom, the bridge that connects heaven's resources with earthly needs. However, it's also the most contested territory in the life of every believer. The moment you begin to shift from being a consumer of God's blessings to becoming a distributor of His resources, you enter a battleground. This is not a physical battleground, but a spiritual one—one where the stakes are high, and the prize is your faith.

The enemy understands that without faith, it is impossible to please God. *(Hebrews 11:6)*. If he can weaken your faith, he can cripple your ability to access the authority and power that come with being a Kingdom distributor. This is why the battle for your faith is relentless, and it's also why understanding this battle is crucial to your growth in Kingdom authority.

Let's dive into the strategies the enemy uses to attack your faith, how to recognize the signs of spiritual warfare, and most importantly, how to fight the good fight of faith so that you can move from being a mere consumer to a powerful distributor of God's blessings.

FAITH: THE FOUNDATION OF KINGDOM DISTRIBUTION

The shift from consumer to distributor starts with faith. Faith is the substance that activates the promises of God in your life. Hebrews 11:1 (TLB) tells us,

> *"What is faith? It is the confident assurance that something we want is going to happen. It is the certainty that what we hope for is waiting for us, even though we cannot see it up ahead."*

Consider a farmer who plants seeds in the ground. He cannot see what is happening beneath the soil, but he waters the seed daily with the expectation of a future harvest. This is faith in action. Similarly, as a Kingdom distributor, you plant seeds of faith through your alignment, prayers, words and declarations, praise and worship, giving, generosity, service, and obedience to God's instructions. However, just as the farmer faces challenges like drought, pests, and storms, you will face challenges in your faith journey. The key is to remain undistracted, steadfast, and immoveable as you press on towards the goal of a fruitful harvest.

THE ENEMY'S TACTIC: DELAYS, DOUBTS, AND DISTRACTIONS

The tactic of delay is among one of the most successful strategies of the enemies' in the fight for your faith. When God seems to be slow to respond to your prayers, the enemy uses that waiting time to sow seeds of doubt and discouragement. You begin to doubt whether God really heard your prayers, if you are still in line with His will, or if you have the power to bring about the desired effect from your petitions.

Though it's natural to be doubtful in such times, keep in mind that a delay is not a refusal. Often part of God's preparatory process are delays. One especially good example is Abraham.

Though he expected a son and a large legacy, he waited 25 years for Isaac to be born. Abraham experienced times of uncertainty and even committed blunders throughout that period, yet God's promise stayed clear.

His faith, polished and developed over the protracted wait, finally positioned him as the father of nations. Like Abraham, the waiting season is typically one in which God is developing your character, faith, and endurance. The enemy knows how important this waiting time is. Should he be able to capitalize on your annoyance during these delays, he will erode your will and drive you away from your Kingdom distribution call.

Distractions present themselves as pressing chores, annoyances, or even good possibilities incompatible with God's intention for your life. Anxiety and annoyance can quickly seep in and encourage you to abandon God's timing and stray from His direction. One further tactic of the opponent is wearing you down with harassment. He causes distractions and problems that are meant to wear you out. His aim is to leave you so tired that you miss your spiritual beginning into power, which is what could have been your point of access into more Kingdom authority and effectiveness.

Rather than live as the distributor God has called you to be, his ultimate desire is to make you a perpetual consumer continually seeking signs, miracles, and power. Standing strong throughout seasons of delay requires a recognition of this strategy.

The enemy will use all manner of persecution to create distractions so you can be weary. His goal is to ensure you are so worn out that you miss **the spiritual prom** - the
initiation into spiritual power - afterwhich he desires that you become a chronic consumer and beggar of power, sign, and miracles.

THE MARATHON OF FAITH

Faith is often described as a race, but it's more like a marathon than a sprint. Though in practice it's more of a marathon than a sprint, faith is sometimes defined as a sprint. The runner in a marathon must negotiate highs and lows. Every stride becomes a struggle when the runner feels as though they could keep running indefinitely; then, there are times when tiredness sets in. Times the finish line appears far off, and the desire to give up might be strong.

Experienced marathoners, however, understand that finishing the race is not determined by starting speed. It's about how they fight through the difficult, agonizing sections of the road. In the walk of faith, too, there are seasons of spiritual strength, times when prayers are answered rapidly and everything seems to be in line. The future seems brilliant, and you feel as though you are just where God wants you to be. Like in a marathon, though, there are seasons of tiredness when God seems silent and the promises He promised seem far off.

The fight for your faith gets more intense at these times. One starts to doubt and finds great temptation to give up on God's timing. These are the years, nevertheless, when faith really blossoms. To fulfill God's promises, you have to go past uncertainty and delays, much as the marathon runner keeps on despite tiredness. The apostle Paul grasped this really well. He so pushed Timothy to "fight the good fight of faith." The fight is spiritual rather than physical; it calls for tenacity, perseverance, and a relentless attention on the finish line.

Faith is not about a sprint to the finish, when everything comes naturally. It's about the lengthy, difficult stretches when nothing seems to be happening yet you still believe God's process. It's in those demanding seasons when your faith grows firmly ingrained and when your reliance on God is tested and reinforced. Though you might not see the answers right away, much as a marathon runner's endurance gets them to the finish line, faith's tenacity is the key to releasing God's promises.

This fight is not a physical one but a spiritual battle that requires persistence, endurance, and a focus on the finish line.

RECOGNIZING SPIRITUAL WARFARE

Spiritual warfare is real, and it intensifies when you begin to shift from being a consumer to a distributor. As you grow in your Kingdom authority, the enemy will not sit back idly. He will attack your faith through various means —sowing seeds of doubt, orchestrating delays, and bringing distractions. The purpose of these attacks is to get you to give up on the promises of God. Ephesians 6:12 (TLB) reminds us,

> *"For we are not fighting against people made of flesh and blood, but against persons without bodies—the evil rulers of the unseen world, those mighty satanic beings and great evil princes of darkness who rule this world; and against huge numbers of wicked spirits in the spirit world."*

This means that the battle you face is not just a battle of circumstances but a spiritual war over your faith.

When you face delays in answered prayer, recognize that it is not because God is indifferent. Often, these delays are spiritual battles that require persistence in prayer and unwavering faith. In *Daniel 10*, we see an example of this when Daniel's prayers were delayed for 21 days because of spiritual warfare. The angel eventually came to Daniel and explained that his prayer had been heard from the first day, but a spiritual battle in the heavens had caused the delay.

Peter doubted the initial word that Christ gave him. He saw the persecution.

> *'Peter shouted out, "Lord, if it's really you, then have me join you on the water!" "Come and join me," Jesus replied. Then Peter got down out of the boat, walked on the water and came toward Jesus. But when he saw the wind, he was afraid and, beginning*

to sink, cried out, "Lord, save me!"'
– Matthew 14:28-29 TPT

The wind was boisterous and that is what satan has been using against believers. Satan knows exactly what works on you and he is not going to change it until he find out that what has been working is no longer working.

Jesus implied that 'I saw the warfare but you did not think that coming to Me was warfare.' The enemy releases a mental warfare using physical situations and circumstances to create mental torture that will eventually lead to both physical and spiritual failure.

Peter stepped out of the boat by faith, in faith and on faith, and was walking. But doubt came. The enemy brought a warfare and used doubt. Jesus did not say "why did you let **satan** win?". Instead Jesus said, "why did you let **doubt** win?"

Doubt is when your mind and your whole soul begins to concentrate on your situations and circumstances more than the ability of God to bring you out of those situations and circumstances.

What makes doubt stronger is when you start thinking the situations and circumstances are just confronting you because of you. When you say to yourself "there must be something bigger than me. Walking on this water is not for me alone but for the other disciples and future disciples/believers. The moment you start thinking differently, you start upgrading yourself.

HOW TO FIGHT THE GOOD FIGHT OF FAITH

Sustaining your faith is a conscious fight. Faith takes action and intentionality. So how do you fight the good fight of faith? Here are a few practical steps:

1. **Anchor Your Faith in God's Word:** Faith comes by hearing, and hearing by the word of God.

"Faith, then, is birthed in a heart that responds to God's anointed utterance of the Anointed One".
                    – Romans 10:17 TPT

When doubt creeps in, return to the promises of God in His word. Remind yourself of His faithfulness throughout history and in your own life.

2.   **Persist in Prayer:** Just because your answer has nott arrived does not mean it is not on the way. In *Luke 18:1-8,* Jesus shares the parable of the persistent widow, teaching us to always pray and not give up. Persistence in prayer is a weapon in the fight of faith.

3.   **Surround Yourself with Faith-filled People:** The company you keep can either strengthen or weaken your faith. Surround yourself with people who will encourage you to stay the course, pray with you, and remind you of God's promises.

4.   **Praise in the Waiting:** Praise is a powerful weapon. It shifts your focus from your problems to the greatness of God. In *Acts 16,* Paul and Silas were in prison, yet they chose to praise God in the midst of their chains. As a result, a miracle happened, and they were set free.

5.   **Stay Aligned with God's Will:** Remember the lessons from Chapter Two on consecration and alignment. When you are aligned with God's will, even in seasons of delay, you can trust that He is working all things together for your good. – *Romans 8:28*

The battle for your faith is intense because the prize is great. When you fight the good fight of faith, you position yourself as a distributor of God's resources, not just a consumer. Your faith not only unlocks the promises of God for your life but also makes you a conduit through which others can receive His blessings.

Remember, the enemy is after your faith because he knows that a faith-filled believer is a dangerous threat to his kingdom. But as you persist in faith, holding on to God's promises even in the face of delays, doubts, and distractions, you will experience the fullness of Kingdom authority. You will move from being a consumer to a distributor—one who carries the power and presence of God into every area of life.

In the end, the fight of faith is worth it, for as Paul declares in 2 Timothy 4:7-8 (TPT),

> "...There's a crown of righteousness waiting in heaven for me, and I know that my Lord will reward me on his day of righteous judgment."

That crown is not just for Paul; it is for every believer who endures the battle for their faith and stands firm in the promises of God.

CHAPTER 4

OPERATING IN SPIRITUAL AUTHORITY

"And I have given you authority over all the power of the Enemy, and to walk among serpents and scorpions and to crush them. Nothing shall injure you!"

– Luke 10:19 TLB

To truly transition from a consumer to a distributor in the Kingdom of God, you must understand and operate in the spiritual authority that has been granted to you. Without this authority, you cannot fulfill your divine mandate or effectively impact the world. The Kingdom of God operates on principles of authority, and as a believer, you are called to exercise that authority.

It's important that we explore and understand what it means to operate in spiritual authority, how to recognize the power you possess in Christ, and how to overcome the tactics of the enemy.

The power and the authority that the Church of Christ is ordained to live in is so mind blowing. If at this stage, you are not excited about the kingdom, most likely something has corrupted your soul in the spirit realm. The excitement about the kingdom is the fact that we belong to a Kingdom of power and we are in the very last phase of everything where God is about to demonstrate His highest power though the church.

The Source of Spiritual Authority

The foundation of spiritual authority lies in the finished work of Jesus Christ. When Christ died on the cross and rose again, He defeated the powers of darkness and reclaimed authority over all things. In Matthew 28:18 (TLB), Jesus declared,

"I have been given all authority in heaven and earth."

As believers, we are not left powerless. Through our union with Christ, we share in His authority and are empowered to operate as distributors of His power on earth.

It is important to understand that the authority we walk in is not our own. Just like a police officer has authority not because of who he is personally but because of the government he represents, we operate in spiritual authority because we represent the King of Kings. When a police officer raises his hand to stop traffic, people respond because they recognize the authority behind him. Similarly, when you apply the Word of God, command circumstances, or resist the enemy in Jesus' name, you do so under the authority of Christ.

In *Luke 10:19*, Jesus told His disciples, "I have given you authority to trample on snakes and scorpions and to overcome all the power of the enemy; nothing will harm you." **This was not just for the twelve apostles but for every believer who operates under the Lordship of Christ.** Jesus gave this authority to empower us to advance His Kingdom and to over come the enemy's schemes.

Understanding Your Position in Christ

To effectively operate in spiritual authority, you must first recognize your position in Christ. Ephesians 2:6 (TPT) tells us that

"He raised us up with Christ the exalted One, and we ascended with him into the glorious perfection and authority of the heavenly realm, for we are now co-seated as one with Christ!."

This means that as believers, we are seated with Christ in a position of authority, far above principalities, powers, and all the forces of darkness.

Many Christians struggle to walk in authority because they are unaware of their identity in Christ. If you see yourself as a weak, powerless Christian, you will never operate in the authority that is rightfully yours. The enemy thrives on ignorance. He knows that as long as you are unaware of the authority you have, he can continue to wreak havoc in your life, unchecked. However, when you understand that you are seated with Christ in the heavenly realms, you begin to see yourself as God sees you—a co-heir with Christ, empowered to enforce His victory on earth. This mindset shift is crucial in transitioning **from a consumer mentality** (one who waits passively for God's blessings) **to a distributor mentality** (one who actively enforces God's will on earth).

EXERCISING AUTHORITY OVER THE ENEMY

Spiritual power is given to believers so that they can rule over the enemy. This is one of the main reasons for this. As we read Luke 10:19, Jesus makes it clear that He has given us the power to walk on snakes and scorpions, which are symbols of evil spirits and all kinds of spiritual resistance. John 10:10 says it's very clear what the enemy wants to do: he comes to steal, kill, and destroy.

He wants to get in the way of you reaching your goals and get in your way. Despite this, it is important to remember that he is an enemy that has been defeated and that his power is weak compared to the power that Christians have in Christ.

Jesus said,

> *"A thief has only one thing in mind—he wants to steal, slaughter, and destroy. But I have come to give you everything in abundance, more than you expect —life in its fullness until you overflow!"*
> – Matthew 10:10 TPT

Jesus has given us everything we need, not just to meet our basic needs but also to thrive in perfect plenty. This promise is a reminder of that. It's a problem, though, that many believers don't follow through with this power in its entirety. There's no problem with the enemy having power over Christians; the problem is that many believers don't use the power they have over him.

Take the example of a king who has all the power he needs to rule his kingdom but doesn't want to use it. As a result, he lets an enemy take over the kingdom. This is exactly what happens when Christians let fear, doubt, or other things get in the way of using the power that Christ has given them. Our instructions tell us to overcome these problems and show the power that God has given us.

THE BATTLE FOR AUTHORITY: RECOGNIZING THE ENEMY'S TACTICS

> *"He will defy the Most High God and wear down the saints with persecution, and he will try to change all laws, morals, and customs."*
> – Daniel 7:25 TLB

Our enemy uses a very strong strategy to wear out the saints by trying to destroy the very core of a believer's faith and power. However, this strategy has not become less successful over time, even though it has been used since the beginning of time. The enemy's main goal is to weaken the spiritual strength and confidence of God's people by attacking them on many levels, including their minds, feelings, and spirits.

False information, giving up, and keeping you from focusing are the three tools that the enemy uses to attack. These tools are carefully chosen to make Christians doubt their own power in Christ. This power is seen by the enemy as a strong force that poses a major threat to them. These powers were given to them by Jesus Himself. In Luke 10:19, it says, "Behold, I have given you power to walk on snakes and scorpions and over all the enemy's strength, and nothing will hurt you." By attacking over and over, the enemy is trying to weaken this power so that he can complete his own plans. As soon as a Christian starts to use the spiritual power that God has given them, the enemy's plans to harm them become very clear.

These people are being targeted not by chance but on purpose because the enemy knows that an authoritative believer could hurt his kingdom. When a saint is fully in charge of their spiritual life, they are like a spiritual fighter who is armed and dangerous to the forces of evil. The fact that this is true shows how important it is to stay alert and have a strong faith in Christ, since the struggle gets worse as people get better at working in the Kingdom. Distractions are one of the most sneaky and effective things that the enemy does.

The enemy is very good at creating many problems, disputes, and even chances that look like they could be good in order to take a believer's mind off of the heavenly job they have been given. This strategy is especially sneaky because it often looks like progress or success in today's world. This could happen to a Christian who is called to work in business to further God's kingdom but is flooded with lucrative possibilities that, while making them money, have nothing to do with their heavenly calling. The risk comes from the fact that these distractions can slowly pull someone away from their real goal without them being aware of it at first.

You can see a clear picture of how these ideas are used in the journey I have been on in my own walk with the Lord. In the early stages of my calling, the enemy tried to overpower me by throwing a lot of distractions and problems in my way. In contrast, my strong belief in my calling and my strong desire for the Kingdom of God made it impossible for these forces to get through to me. I never even considered giving up on my goal, not even when things were really tough and there was a lot of resistance against me. Instead of being strong because of my own willpower, I was able to handle things well because I had a strong, purposeful relationship with God and knew that He wanted me to serve Him.

The strong support I got from my close relationship with God and my unwavering faith in His Word helped me stay strong during these very hard times. It was easy for me to stand strong in the authority that Christ had given me because these pillars gave me the stability and strength I needed. Ephesians 6:10–11 says, "Finally, be strong in the Lord and in the power of his might." Put on all the armor that God has given you so that you can fight the devil's plans. This verse from the Bible shows where a believer's power to fight the enemy comes from.

My experiences have shown me over and over again how powerful it is to stand on the Bible and use spiritual authority through prayer and public speaking. Through my own experiences, I know that this method can lead to miraculous breakthroughs in situations that look like they can't be solved. When the power of Christ was talked about, resistance would go away, sometimes even before it showed up, and money would come in from places that no one expected. These events were not just random; they were clear proof of God's power working through a Christian who knows and uses their spiritual authority.

As a witness to my life, I can say with confidence that when someone is operating in all of their spiritual power, their enemy has no choice but to run away. This concept is a strong proof that what you say is true. It's not only small groups of people that can access this reality. Anyone who believes Christ and walks in the power He has bestowed upon them can access it. Ephesians 6:12 reminds us that our struggle is against celestial spiritual forces of evil rather than against humans of this planet. Those who believe in God should keep in mind that if we remain strong in the power God has given us, we can conquer any obstacle and progress in the Kingdom of God with unflinching resolve and efficiency.

AUTHORITY IN ACTION: THE POWER OF COMMANDING

The enemy uses a strong and tried-and-true method to wear down the saints: he tries to weaken their faith and ability to do good. Even though it's old, this plan to hurt God's people still works. There are many ways that the enemy tries to hurt Christians' minds, feelings, and spirits in order to break down their spiritual will and faith. The enemy's triangle is made up of lies, discouragement, and distraction. These are all meant to make Christians doubt their God-given authority in Christ. The enemy sees this as a big threat to his power because it gives Jesus power.

"Behold, I have given you authority to tread on serpents and scorpions, and over all the power of the enemy, and nothing shall hurt you," says Luke 10:19. The enemy's constant attacks are meant to weaken this strength, making it harder for Christians to move God's kingdom forward. The enemy focuses all of their efforts on believers as soon as they start to use their spiritual power. That's because the enemy knows that a powerful believer could hurt his realm, so this targeting is planned and not random.

When a saint is fully in charge of their spiritual life, they are like a spiritual warrior, armed and dangerous to the forces of evil. This fact makes it even more important to always be alert and firmly rooted in Christ, because the spiritual fight gets tougher as you become more effective in the Kingdom. Interruptions are one of the sneakiest things an enemy can do. The enemy loves to bombard believers with events, arguments, and even what seem like good chances that take their attention away from their holy duty. In the real world, this is a sign of success or progress, so it's particularly smart.

For instance, a Christian who is called to spread God's kingdom in the business world might be flooded with many lucrative opportunities that don't have much to do with their holy mission. The risk comes from how hard these distractions are to avoid. Over time, they can lead someone astray from their goal without them realizing it. These ideas have been very useful to me in my work as a minister.

Early in my calling, there were times when the enemy tried to break me down by throwing a lot of distractions and problems at me. But my strong trust in my calling and my deep love for God's kingdom stood in the way of these demands. Even when things were very hard and there weren't enough things, I never thought about giving up on my goal. This strength came from a deliberate, deep relationship with God and a clear understanding of my divine calling as His servant. During these hard times, two things held me down: my close relationship with God and my strong foundation in His Word. These pillars gave me the safety and strength I needed to stand firm in the strength Christ gave me.

"Finally, be strong in the Lord and in the power of his might," Ephesians 6:10–11 tells us. If you put on all of God's weapons, you might be able to stop the devil's plans. This book shows how a believer can protect themselves from threats from the enemy. Over and over again, my life has shown me how powerful it is to stand on God's Word and use spiritual authority through prayer and promises. I have seen firsthand how this method can lead to amazing findings in situations that don't seem possible. When Christ's power was used, money would come in from places no one expected it, and resistance would go away, sometimes before it even started.

The proof in my life is very strong that when someone uses their spiritual power fully, the enemy has no choice but to back off. This truth will be open to everyone who believes in Christ and obeys His commands. Christians should remember that our battle is not against people but against the heavenly forces of evil in the sky (Ephesians 6:12). We can overcome any problem and move the Kingdom of God forward with unwavering effectiveness if we stay strong in the power that God has given us.

THE AUTHORITY OF A POLICE OFFICER

The authority of a believer can be compared to that of a police officer. When a police officer raises his hand to stop traffic, the vehicles obey not because of the officer's physical strength but because of the authority vested in him by the government. Similarly, as believers, we have been vested with the authority of heaven. When you speak, the spiritual realm must respond—not because of who you are, but because of who you represent.

However, just like a police officer who fails to exercise his authority will be ineffective, a believer who fails to use their spiritual authority will be powerless against the enemy. Authority unused is authority wasted. It's time to rise up and take your place as a Kingdom distributor, enforcing God's will on earth through the authority He has given you.

THE ROLE OF FAITH IN EXERCISING AUTHORITY

Operating in spiritual authority requires faith. Without

faith, it is impossible to please God.

> *"You can never please God without faith, without depending on him. Anyone who wants to come to God must believe that there is a God and that he rewards those who sincerely look for him."*
> – Hebrews 11:6 TLB

Walking in the fullness of your spiritual power requires a strong and continuous trust. This faith is the key that unlocks the vast possibilities of the authority bestowed upon followers of Christ. When dealing with illness, commanding financial support, or ordering demonic forces to go, you must truly believe that your words have the full weight and power of heaven itself. In Mark 11:23 (AMP), Jesus accentuated this concept:

In *Mark 11:23 (AMP)*, Jesus said,

> *"I assure you and most solemnly say to you, whoever says to this mountain, 'Be lifted up and thrown into the sea!' and does not doubt in his heart [in God's unlimited power], but believes that what he says is going to take place, it will be done for him [in accordance with God's will].*

This book highlights the type of faith required to effectively exercise spiritual authority—a strong, unwavering faith that knows with confidence that orders issued in Jesus' name must be carried out. Such faith is neither purely intellectual nor passive. Believers in this active, living faith are motivated to speak with authority because they fully expect to see tangible results. This level of trust recognizes that God's limitless power, working through those who believe, will move mountains, both literal and symbolic, rather than human ability. Along my own road with God, I've witnessed the transformative power of this type of faith.

Having been presented with seemingly insurmountable obstacles, I have had to bravely believe God's promises above impossible conditions. Whether it was praying for health, ordering financial breakthroughs, or handling demonic opposition, I have seen the extraordinary emerge as I used the power Christ assigned to me. I can think of one really compelling case. We ran into major financial difficulties early in my employment, which could have put an end to our work. Rather than succumb to uncertainty or concern, I resolved to exercise the authority God had put upon me and keep His promises.

I spoke provision into life with unwavering faith, commanding the means we needed to manifest. Days later, we were blessed with unexpected gifts and opportunities that not only met our immediate needs but also began us on a path of steady improvement. Among many other encounters, this one taught me that walking in spiritual authority is not about personal power or charm. It's about coordinating our beliefs with God's will and communicating with the confidence that comes from understanding we have the full support of heaven.

In the face of contradicting facts, this faith—which holds in mind the invisible reality of God's kingdom—remains constant. Developing this degree of faith and power requires constant exercise in spiritual authority, a dynamic prayer life, and consistent immersion in God's Word, I have come to see. As we develop in Christ and the power He has bestowed upon us lets us organically ascend and enable us to see more important outcomes and speak more freely.

OVERCOMING FEAR AND INTIMIDATION

One of the enemy's primary tactics to keep believers from operating in spiritual authority is fear and intimidation. He knows that if he can get you to question your authority or doubt your ability to exercise it, he can keep you bound. But the Word of God declares in *2 Timothy 1:7 (KJV),*

> *"For God has not given us a spirit of fear, but of power and of love and of a sound mind."*

Fear is a thief that robs you of your authority. When you give in to fear, you allow the enemy to have the upper hand. However, when you confront fear with the truth of God's Word, it loses its grip. You must remind yourself daily that you have been given authority over all the power of the enemy, and nothing shall by any means harm you *(Luke 10:19).*

WALKING IN CONTINUOUS AUTHORITY

The essence of walking in spiritual power and authority is a lifetime habit requiring deliberate development rather than a one-time encounter. You must have a close, personal connection with God, be securely anchored in His Word, and be especially sensitive to the direction of the Holy Spirit if you are to keep walking continuously in this authority.

This spiritual awareness is analogous to a soldier's constant preparedness for combat; we, too, must be spiritually prepared to employ our God-given strength at any time. Mark 11:23 (AMP) emphasizes this principle: "I assure you and most solemnly say to you, whoever says to this mountain, 'Be lifted up and thrown into the sea!' and does not doubt in his heart [in God's unlimited power], but believes that what he says will be done for him [in accordance with God's will]."

On my personal journey, frequent spiritual power exercises have transformed me. There were times when it appeared that I was confronting insurmountable challenges, but with unwavering faith and the proclaiming of God's promises, I witnessed incredible transformations. Speaking with heavenly authority has frequently demonstrated God's might in concrete ways, whether in financial crises, physical concerns, or ministry challenges.

As one's relationship with God grows and they employ His delegated power on a daily basis, they experience substantial changes. You go from being a passive recipient of God's blessings to a powerful vehicle for His Kingdom resources. This growth is about becoming an agent of divine influence and impact in all aspects of life, not just for personal gain. Regular Bible study, a vibrant prayer life, and practical faith application are all essential for developing this level of spiritual influence. These disciplines help us to strengthen our faith, sharpen our spiritual sensitivities, and speak more freely and eloquently.

This is ultimately the life God has called us to—one of significant impact, widespread influence, and consistent success. We enter the fullness of our divine calling by fully embracing and exercising our spiritual authority, converting ourselves into powerful tools for God's kingdom on Earth.

CHAPTER 5

THE ENEMY'S STRATEGY: BLOCKING ANSWERS

"But for twenty-one days the mighty Evil Spirit who overrules the kingdom of Persia blocked my way. Then Michael, one of the top officers of the heavenly army, came to help me, so that I was able to break through these spirit rulers of Persia.."

– Daniel 10:13 TLB

In the journey from being a consumer of God's blessings to becoming a distributor of His Kingdom resources, understanding the spiritual dynamics at play is crucial. One of the most common challenges believers face in their walk with God is the apparent delay in the answers to their prayers. Many times, it seems as though the heavens are silent, and God is slow to respond. But what if the delay is not on God's part? What if the enemy is actively working to block the answers that have already been dispatched from Heaven?

As we journey on, we will explore the enemy's strategy of blocking answers to your prayers, the purpose behind his tactics, and how to push through in persistent prayer and consecration to receive what God has already prepared for you. The truth is, the enemy is fully aware of the authority you carry as a distributor of God's Kingdom, and his primary objective is to stop you from accessing and releasing that power. You must be aware of his tactics in order to overcome and triumph.

UNDERSTANDING THE ENEMY'S TACTICS: SPIRITUAL RESISTANCE

We can better understand Daniel's spiritual struggle by praying all the time. This story explains how the invisible worlds affect our lives on Earth. This chapter from Daniel 10:13 helps us reflect on how our prayers and the spiritual forces that surround us interact in intricate ways. Daniel fasted and prayed for twenty-one days straight because he was determined to find God's will. His continuous commitment demonstrates the importance of patience as we seek spiritual growth. On the other hand, Daniel was unable to see the immediate impact of his prayers on the celestial world.

According to Daniel 10:12, Daniel's words were heard, and a reaction began the moment he chose to learn and be humble before God. He did not receive an immediate response to his prayer, but this was not due to God's unwillingness or indifference to addressing it. But it was sparked by a powerful spiritual struggle that was taking place outside of human sight. It was a cosmic struggle between a demon linked to Satan's army, the "prince of the Persian kingdom," and the angel who delivered God's message. This duel lasted for the whole 21-day contest. The spiritual struggle had an immediate impact on the physical world; therefore, God's response to Daniel took longer than expected.

The barrier was finally broken through with the assistance

of the Archangel Michael, who is regarded as one of God's most powerful angels. So, thanks to this divine intervention, Daniel received the answer, tipping the balances in favor of God's message. There is further evidence that spiritual battle occurs and that heavenly entities play an important part in carrying out God's purpose on earth due to the abrupt change of circumstances. This Bible narrative emphasizes a very real and active part that interacts with our real world rather than being just an idea. Many Christians forget about this fact. The invisible forces are constantly at work. Some seek to carry out God's plans, while others try to prevent them.

These spiritual creatures are at odds with one another and fighting wars, which may have a direct impact on what happens to us and how we react to it in our daily lives. Their opponent in this mental battle is both intelligent and cunning. Satan and his agents attempt to erode believers' faith by causing delays and other hardships. To achieve their objectives, they try to discourage people from praying all the time and raise questions about God's faithfulness. The enemy's goal in making us wait is to weaken our confidence and divert our attention away from the crucial role God has assigned us in His kingdom.

Realizing this helps one comprehend the importance of praying every day. We are not simply following a religious practice or measuring how long we can go; we are utilizing our most essential spiritual tool. We actively support the spiritual battles being fought for us as long as we pray frequently. When the enemy attempts to thwart God's intentions for our lives, our unwavering faith and dedication defend us exceptionally well. Also, this story allows us to see things from a different perspective while we are waiting for God or when it appears that God is not communicating to us.

Even if it appears that nothing is going on, there may be

a lot of spiritual activity going on beneath the surface. It's possible that the prayers we say are causing spiritual events we can't see, but they're necessary for God's purpose to be carried out in our lives and the world around us. Thinking about this offers us a renewed sense of enthusiasm and determination when we pray. If we feel that our prayers are being heard and that supernatural forces are working for us, we may be motivated to continue praying even if we do not see immediate results. This serves as a reminder that if we give up too soon, we risk missing out on the next big discovery.

THE POWER OF PERSISTENT PRAYER

One of the enemy's most effective strategies is to **introduce weariness during a season of waiting**. He knows that if he can make you tired, discouraged, or distracted, you will be tempted to give up. But persistent prayer is **your counter-strategy.** Jesus, knowing the importance of persistence, shared the parable of the persistent widow in *Luke 18:1-8.* In this story, the widow kept coming to the unjust judge, demanding justice. Eventually, the judge granted her request, not because of righteousness, but because of her persistence.

Jesus concludes the parable with a powerful question: "When the Son of Man comes, will He really find faith on the earth?"

> *"God will give swift justice to those who don't give up. So be ever praying, ever expecting, in the same way as the widow."*
> – Luke 18:8 TPT

The question speaks directly to the issue of enduring faith. The enemy's goal is to cause you to lose heart, but Jesus is looking for those who will remain steadfast in faith, even in the face of delays. Like the widow, you must be persistent, continually pressing into God's presence and reminding Heaven that you are not giving up until you see the manifestation of your breakthrough.

Let me share a personal testimony that illustrates the power of unwavering prayer in overcoming the enemy's resistance. While I was on a mission trip to Nigeria, I received a vision about a spiritual daughter of mine who was facing an urgent and life-threatening situation. The details of the vision were clear, and I knew that immediate intercession was required. I initially requested for corporate prayer but the Lord spoke to me and instructed me to intercede on my own as the outcome of this particular matter depended on my intercession and my spirit. Without hesitation, I began to pray fervently. Hours passed, and it seemed as if nothing was changing and the person involved began panicking. But I proceeded to reassuring them of the word of the Lord and I did not stop praying. The situation looked bleak, and if we had relied on what we could see in the natural, it would have been easy to quit. However, in the spirit, I understood that the battle was not against flesh and blood but against principalities and powers. I continued to press in for an answer until suddenly, the breakthrough came. Her situation shifted dramatically within hours, and it became clear that what had been resisted was now released and manifested by the power of God.

This experience reinforced the importance of not giving up, even when it feels like your prayers are hitting a wall or the prophesy seems far from sight or reality. Often, the answer has already been dispatched, but there is resistance in the spiritual realm that must be overcome through persistence in prayer.

THE ENEMY'S AGENDA: WEARING YOU DOWN

"He will defy the Most High God and wear down the saints with persecution, and he will try to change all laws, morals, and customs. God's people will be helpless in his hands for three and a half years."
– Daniel 7:25 TLB

Satan understands the power of a believer who is

persistent and unwavering in their pursuit of God. His strategy, then, is to wear you out.

Daniel 7:25 tells us that the enemy seeks to "wear out the saints of the Most High."

How does he do this? By blocking answers, introducing delays, and planting seeds of doubt in your heart. Imagine a farmer who has sown seeds and is waiting for the harvest. The enemy's goal is to convince that farmer to abandon the field, to believe that no fruit will ever come. He will send droughts, storms, and weeds to discourage the farmer, hoping that in frustration, the farmer will leave the crops untended. In the same way, satan bombards you with distractions, doubts, and delays to make you think your prayers will never be answered.

Satan will use unanswered prayers as a systematic means of discouraging and wearing you. It is a warfare that you have to win. Insist on having results because you are the salt of the earth. If you not do anything about the decadence of the earth, nothing will go right. Everything will decay. Make a decision to think and be the one who knows that a generation is waiting for you so you cannot perish in any situation.

In the story of Jesus commanding the storm to be still, before the Word came, the storm was there. The storm could not stop the power of the word.

Faith: The Driving Force Behind Your Persistence

Though we touched on this in the previous chapter, faith is a vital necessity in your faith work and in overcoming the noisyness of the world. Faith is the fuel that keeps you pressing forward, even when there's resistance.

> "But without faith it is impossible to [walk with God and] please Him, for whoever comes [near] to God must [necessarily] believe that God exists and that

He rewards those who [earnestly and diligently] seek
Him.
— Hebrews 11:6 AMP

Faith is not just believing that God can; it's trusting that He will, in His perfect timing. When the enemy blocks the answers to your prayers, it is your faith that keeps you praying and believing, even when you don't see results immediately.

When Jesus spoke of faith the size of a mustard seed, He was not focusing on the amount of faith but on the persistence of faith.

> *"I promise you, if you have faith inside of you no*
> *bigger than the size of a small mustard seed, you*
> *can say to this mountain, 'Move away from here*
> *and go over there,' and you will see it move! There is*
> *nothing you could not do!"*
> — Matthew 17:20 TPT

A mustard seed is small, but it has the potential to grow into something great. Your faith may seem small in the face of opposition, but as you continue to water it with prayer, it will grow and move the mountains that stand in your way.

BREAKING THROUGH THE BARRIERS

> *"I will give you the keys to God's kingdom. When*
> *you speak judgment here on earth, that judgment*
> *will be God's judgment. When you promise*
> *forgiveness here on earth, that forgiveness*
> *will be God's forgiveness."*
> — Matthew 16:19 ERV

Jesus gives us a **powerful promise** in *Matthew 16:19*. This means that you have the authority to break through the barriers the enemy has set up. When the enemy tries to block your answers, **you have the power** to bind his works and loose the answers that have already been released from Heaven.

When Daniel's answer was delayed, it was not because God had forgotten him; it was because there was spiritual opposition that needed to be overcome. And in the same way, your answer may already be on its way, but the enemy is fighting to prevent its delivery.

It is not enough to wait passively for God to act. As a distributor of Kingdom authority, you must rise up in prayer and declaration, using the authority that has been given to you. Declare the Word of God over your situation, and command the forces of darkness to release what rightfully belongs to you.

THE POWER OF AGREEMENT IN PRAYER

The power of unity and agreement is a spiritual aspect of prayer that is often overlooked but is very important. Synergy happens when Christians work together in harmony and focus their ideas and beliefs on one goal. This unity has the power to move mountains in both the spiritual and physical worlds. Not only is it a nice idea, but praying together as a group is required by the Bible and has clear benefits that can be seen.

In Matthew 18, line 19, Jesus made it clear how important it is for a group to pray. "Again I say to you, that if two believers on earth agree about anything that they ask, it will be done for them by My Father in heaven." He told you. Christ's word shows the two-way power that comes from Christians praying together with their hearts and voices. When all of our prayers are put together, they create a psychic resonance that reaches higher into the sky. It looks like this is the case. When you're having trouble with your prayer life, you need to know that you don't have to fight every war by yourself.

It can make a difference in your life to find other believers who share your views and back them up. People who pray with you should be firmly rooted in the Bible and have a mature view of spiritual battle. Their prayer relationship with you can give you the extra spiritual force you need to get past things that seem impossible to get past. Because of Daniel's story, we can see this idea clearly at work in the spiritual world.

As things turned out, the Archangel Michael's presence tipped the scales in favor of God's message, allowing Daniel to hear the answer to his plea. The fact that other Christians are praying with us probably serves the same purpose in our lives. Their prayers, along with ours, could be the push we need to beat the resistance and make the breakthrough we've been waiting for. This idea that prayer can help people understand each other goes beyond two people. When more people come to pray together, there are a lot more chances for spiritual growth.

This sets off a mental tsunami that completely overwhelms the opponent's defenses. This is one reason why business prayer events, prayer chains, and even worldwide prayer movements can be very helpful. Every new voice that joins the prayer chorus puts more spiritual pressure on evil forces. Still, it's important to remember that the number of people who show up doesn't tell you everything you need to know about how well the degree of agreement works in prayer. How strong the agreement is is just as important as how many people agree with it.

When picking people to pray with, look for those who are rooted in God's Word, full of faith, and in line with what God wants. Because these people are spiritually mature and well-informed, your prayers will have more power and help you focus on the specific areas where you are facing resistance. In this spiritual fight, it is very important to know exactly how the other person is coming at you. Satan's main goals are to make you give up by making you wait a long time, to stop you from getting replies to your prayers, and to finally lose your faith.

Satan will have accomplished a great victory if he can bring you down to the point where you can't pray. But as a Kingdom agent, you are called to a higher purpose. You were given psychic power so that you can stop their plans in the right way. Believers have this power because Christ gave it to them directly. You can now bind the enemy's actions and let Heaven's remedies work. You shouldn't try to get stronger on your own; instead, you should trust the power and promises that God has given you. It's not that you want answers when you pray this way; you're working with God to show you His plan for the world.

Along with commitment and unwavering trust, the only way to get past problems and find answers is to pray all the time. We give ourselves over to God's will and let Him clean out our hearts and align our wills with His. This is called "consecration." Being close to this person will make your thoughts stronger and more effective. Unwavering trust helps you stay rooted in God's promises, even when things take longer than expected or there seems to be no response. It also stops the enemy from removing doubt in your mind. Praying is a hard fight that shouldn't be taken easily.

Tenacity, endurance, and the ability to stay calm even when it's not clear what will happen right away are all important traits. On the other hand, Christ already offers success to those who choose to fight the good fight of faith. We can't always see the results of our prayers, but every prayer we say with faith has an effect. Remember that, just like Daniel, as soon as you say your prayers, they begin to move things along in the spiritual world. The answers may be on their way to you, no matter what hurdles may be in their way. You need to stay calm, pray, and start to believe that God will keep his word. By being patient, agreeing, and having faith, you will receive revelations and see God's will come true in your life and around you.

CHAPTER 6

THE OVERFLOW OF ABUNDANCE: LIVING BEYOND SURVIVAL

"...I came that they may have and enjoy life, and have it in abundance [to the full, till it overflows]."

– John 10:10 AMP

When Jesus came to Earth, He did not merely come to ensure survival for His people—He came to bring abundance. Kingdom living is not about just getting by; it's about thriving. In this chapter, I will focus on how shifting from a consumer mindset to a distributor mindset positions you for the overflow of God's abundance.

When you begin to live with the understanding that God is a God of abundance, you stop clinging to what you have and start living in a place of overflow where your needs are met, and you have more than enough to bless others.

The widely known principle that "you get more of what you give or release" is deeply rooted in both spiritual and natural laws. It reflects a universal truth that when you sow generously, you reap abundantly. This principle, often referred to as the **Law of Sowing and Reaping,** is prevalent throughout scripture, as well as in everyday life, business, relationships, and personal growth.

Let's dive into an understanding of what abundance means when it come to things of the Kingdom of God.

Understanding Abundance in the Kingdom

Usually limited to quantifiable objects like financial success, material goods, or social level, the idea of abundance in our contemporary, materialistic society is Conversely, this limited viewpoint fails to convey the actual meaning of prosperity as imagined in the Kingdom of God. Declaring He came to give life "to the full," Jesus offers a deep and life-changing insight into this idea in the book of John, chapter 10, verse 10. One cannot simply survive or persevere in the face of persistent hardship if one is to meet the promise of a full life.

On the other hand, it shows a life full of heavenly kindness, relentless happiness, great peace, and plenty of resources in all spheres of our lives. The idea of abundance in the Kingdom transcends mere wealth in money. All aspects of life, including our spiritual, emotional, physical, and—yes, financial health—are blessed by the great richness it offers. It is a richness found in every sphere of life. This plenty is about having everything we need to complete God's particular purpose for our life, as well as a surplus that enables us to assist others on their paths; it is not only about having enough to meet our own wants.

We experience God's provision in ways much beyond what money can purchase in this state of flourishing rather than plain survival. When we start to view ourselves as carriers of God's benefits instead of consumers, we are undergoing a major paradigm change. This change in viewpoint helps us to recognize that God's wealth is meant to last, not just with us. We are conduits through which His compassion pours, therefore affecting individuals and clearly visiblely advancing His kingdom on Earth; we are not that end goal for His benefits.

This distribution perspective helps us to match God's giving heart and His will to reach out and help others via us. We thus participate actively in God's great plan of redemption and atonement. Seeing the great difference between consumers and distributors in the Kingdom is shocking and exposing. Consumers make selections about what to buy depending on scarcity; they are always fascinated with self-preservation and gain. Fearing there won't be enough, they grab to what they have with all their strength. Conversely, distributors are quite aware of a spiritual principle according to which God replenishes more the more they provide.

This is a great truth about the character of God's economic system, not a straightforward "prosperity gospel" message. Whether it be possessions, time, skills, or love, as we let go of what God has given us, we create space for God to pour much more into our lives. This idea encourages us to live a life of giving driven by faith by challenging our natural inclinations. We have to first see our relationship with God and the tools He provides from the standpoint of a distributor, therefore developing the attitude of one.

This means realizing that God, not humans, is the ultimate source of all supplies. This understanding releases us from the tension and anxiety associated with trying to support ourselves and opens us to the infinite wealth God has to provide. We see a divine cycle of release and replenishment as we carefully divide what He has sent to us: giving and multiplying, planting and harvesting. This cycle covers all aspects of our lives where God's glory may be shown and shared, not only the advantages of financial circumstances. Beyond physical possessions, the idea of riches in the kingdom transcends that as well.

The idea holds true for all of our resources—including time, talents, knowledge, love, and spiritual gifts. We understand that God always renews and increases our capacity to give as we so freely share with others. This leads to a beautiful cycle of blessings that not only enhances the quality of our own lives but also significantly and long-term affects the surroundings. It is a tangible portrayal of God's love flooding our lives to affect the lives of others.

Having a distributor attitude does not mean discounting the necessity of judgment or acting without moderation in handling financial problems. Our hearts should be in line with God's giving nature, and we should start trusting Him as our last source. It is about being a good steward of His resources and applying them to improve the quality of life for others while so advancing the long-term growth of His kingdom. This way of approaching life and resources questions the scarcity mindset of society and invites us to lead a life characterized by supernatural impacts and provision.

Adopting a distributor mentality further helps matters by altering our view of the possibilities as well as the difficulties we face. We change our viewpoint from one of obstacles to our own personal comfort or success to one of opportunity to share God's provision and love with others. This change of viewpoint helps us to approach obstacles with confidence, knowing that even in the middle of our problems, we have the ability to be channels for God's gifts to flow to people near by.

Every event thus becomes a chance for ministry and proving God's great grace. Living as a distributor of the kingdom means working with God from the beginning in His work of atonement and restoration. It's about realizing that our lives could be a potent monument to God's goodness and provision and that we have been privileged to be able to bless others. Adopting this mindset helps us to fully enjoy life as Jesus promised. This is a life of abundance, influence, and purpose that permeates not only ourselves but also flows through us to a planet in need.

THE MINDSET SHIFT: FROM SCARCITY TO OVERFLOW

One of the biggest obstacles to living in abundance is a

scarcity mindset. This mindset tells you that there is not enough to go around, so you must hold on tightly to whatever you receive. But God is not limited by earthly resources.

> *"I am convinced that my God will fully satisfy every*
> *need you have, for I have seen the abundant riches*
> *of glory revealed to me through Jesus Christ!"*
> – Philippians 4:19 TPT

Notice the phrase *"according to His riches"*—not according to the economy, your salary, or your circumstances.

In order to fully embrace the principle of giving and receiving, you must break free from the consumer mentality that says, "I need to hold on to what I have because there may not be enough." This mentality leads to stagnation and limits what God can do through you.

Ultimately, the principle of getting more of what you give is not just about material blessings; it is about living in the flow of God's abundant provision. When you align yourself with God's heart for giving, you open yourself up to receive all that He has for you.

When you truly believe that God's resources are limitless, you stop operating in fear and start giving freely, knowing that your supply comes from Heaven. This is the first step in moving from a consumer to a distributor. God is looking for those who are willing to let go of their limited view of provision and trust Him to supply more than they can ever ask or imagine.

As a distributor in the Kingdom, you are called to be a conduit of blessing, releasing what God has placed in your hands so that others may be blessed—and in return, you will experience the overflow of God's goodness in every area of your life. The more you give, the more you receive—pressed down, shaken together, and running over.

In *2 Kings 4:1-7,* we find the story of a widow who was in desperate need. Her husband had died, and creditors were coming to take her two sons as slaves to pay off the family's debts. She had nothing left—except a little oil. When she approached the prophet Elisha for help, he did not tell her to simply pray for a miracle. Instead, he instructed her to go to her neighbors and borrow empty jars. She was to pour her small amount of oil into these jars.

Now, this must have sounded ridiculous to the widow. How could such a small amount of oil fill multiple jars? But in obedience, she followed the prophet's instructions. As she began pouring, the oil kept flowing until every jar was filled. The miracle only stopped when there were no more jars to fill.

This story is a powerful illustration of God's abundance. The widow's oil did not run out because she obeyed and trusted in God's provision. The oil overflowed beyond her immediate need, allowing her not only to pay off her debts but to live in abundance with her sons.

The same is true for us today. When we are willing to offer God what we have—no matter how small it may seem —He multiplies it. As distributors of His blessings, we do not operate in lack. Instead, we live in the overflow, where God supplies beyond our wildest expectations.

From Receiving to Distributing: The Overflow Principle

The principle of overflow is simple: the more you give, the more you receive. This is a foundational Kingdom principle, one that runs contrary to the world's way of thinking.

> *"Give away your life; you'll find life given back, but not merely given back—given back with bonus and blessing. Giving, not getting, is the way. Generosity begets generosity."*
>
> – Luke 6:38 MSG

Notice the imagery of *"running over."* **God is not a God of barely enough—He is a God of overflow!** But this overflow is not just for our personal enjoyment; it is meant to be distributed. When you operate with an overflow mindset, you become a conduit of God's blessings, allowing what He pours into your life to flow out into the lives of others.

A few years ago, I met a Christian businessman who had built a successful enterprise. Early in his career, he struggled to get by, and his business was barely surviving. One day, while praying, he felt God impress on his heart to start giving generously—something that seemed impossible at the time, given his financial situation. But he obeyed, giving out of the little he had. As he continued to give, something remarkable happened. Doors of opportunity began to open, clients started to come in unexpectedly, and his business began to grow. Today, this man runs a multi-million-dollar company, and he attributes his success to the principle of living in the overflow. **Instead of clinging to what he had, he chose to become a distributor, and God multiplied his resources in ways he never imagined.** One of the most remarkable aspects of the principle of giving is that you always reap more than you sow. The multiplication of what you release is a divine mystery. Jesus illustrated this beautifully in the Parable of the Sower in *Matthew 13:1-9.* He described how a farmer scattered seed on various types of soil, but when the seed fell on good soil, it produced a harvest—some a hundredfold, some sixty, some thirty times what was sown.

> *"But some fell on good soil and produced a crop that was thirty, sixty, and even a hundred times as much as he had planted. If you have ears, listen!"*
> – Matthew 13:8-9 TLB

This principle holds true in every area of life. If you sow time into mentoring someone, you may receive back wisdom, fulfillment, and even opportunities that multiply far beyond the original investment of time. If you sow generosity in your finances, God has promised to multiply your resources. The return is never in the same measure as the giving—it is always greater.

God's multiplication is not limited to tangible returns. Sometimes what we receive is favor, influence, spiritual gifts, or an increased capacity to handle more. God is not confined by natural limitations; He operates in the realm of supernatural abundance. And when you release what is in your hands, you make room for Him to release what is in His hands.

THE ROLE OF STEWARDSHIP IN ABUNDANCE

Stewardship plays a critical role in operating in the overflow. God entrusts us with resources, but how we manage them determines whether we continue to live in abundance or fall back into scarcity. In the parable of the talents (*Matthew 25:14-30*), Jesus tells the story of a master who entrusted his servants with varying amounts of money. The servants who invested and multiplied what they were given were rewarded, while the one who hid his talent out of fear was reprimanded.

> *"But his master replied, 'Wicked man! Lazy slave! Since you knew I would demand your profit, you should at least have put my money into the bank so I could have some interest. Take the money from this man and give it to the man with the $10,000. For the man who uses well what he is given shall be given more, and he shall have abundance. But from the man who is unfaithful, even what little responsibility he has shall be taken from him. And throw the useless servant out into outer darkness: there shall be weeping and gnashing of teeth."*
> – Matthew 25:26-30 TLB

This parable teaches us that God rewards those who are good stewards of His resources. When we use what He gives us wisely—whether it is our time, money, talents, or opportunities—He increases our capacity. But if we hoard what we have been given out of fear or selfishness, we lose out on the greater blessings He wants to release into our lives.

OVERFLOW FOR KINGDOM ADVANCEMENT

Living in the overflow is not just about personal gain; it is about Kingdom advancement. **God blesses us so that we can bless others.** When you live in the overflow, you become a resource for the Kingdom, distributing God's blessings to those in need. Your overflow touches lives, transforms communities, and expands the reach of the Gospel.

> "...there was warm fellowship among all the believers, and no poverty—for all who owned land or houses sold them and brought the money to the apostles to give to others in need."
> – Acts 4:34-35 TLB

Imagine a church where every member lived in the overflow—where no one was in lack because everyone was giving, serving, and distributing the blessings they had received. That is what the early Church looked like in *Acts 4:32-35,* where the believers shared everything they had, and "there were no needy persons among them." This is the power of Kingdom synergy and the overflow principle in action.

During the 2020 global pandemic, many churches faced financial challenges due to lockdowns and restrictions. Our church, Church on Fire International (COFI), despite the economic worries and projections, made a bold decision to give away food and essential supplies to the community through our food pantry. We became the only food pantry in the community and one of the top food haven for families in the Chicagoland area. Week after week, we distributed a variety of groceries, masks, hand sanitizers, toiletries, and even financial assistance to struggling families. We even held more church services than we had ever help and kept our doors open 24 hours for those who needed counseling or a safe place to worship. As a result, COFI has become known as a beacon of hope in the community, and God has provided, preserved, and blessed us in miraculous ways, even leading to us being mortgage-free today with a completely paid off multi-million-dollar headquarters building. What began as a seemingly risky step of faith has turned into a story of overflow and abundance. COFI has discovered that as we gave, God opened the floodgates of Heaven, and we have received more than we have ever imagined.

Living in overflow starts with you. As you transition from being a consumer to a distributor, **remember this:**
ABUNDANCE IS YOUR PORTION. You were not called to survive but to thrive in the Kingdom of God. The shift starts with your mindset.

When you trust God as your source, let go of the scarcity mentality, and live as a distributor, the overflow of His abundance will follow. And through that overflow, you will not only have enough for yourself but more than enough to fulfill your Kingdom assignment and bless others in the process.

CHAPTER 7

WALKING IN FULLNESS: BECOMING THE SOLUTION

"The created world itself can hardly wait for what's coming next."

– Romans 8:19 MSG

We were never meant to live as consumers of miracles, constantly waiting for breakthroughs, handouts, or spiritual interventions. The calling on your life as a child of God is far greater than that. You are not just here to survive, hoping for God to come through—you are here to thrive as a distributor of God's resources, power, and miracles. When you step into the fullness of who you are in Christ, you stop being a passive participant and become an active solution to the world's problems.

Let us explores what it means to walk in the fullness of God's calling, transforming from someone in need into a person who **meets the needs of others.**

THE WAITING CREATION: A WORLD IN NEED OF SOLUTIONS

UNLEASHING KINGDOM AUTHORITY

All of creation is waiting with eager expectation for the sons and daughters of God to be revealed.

> *"For [even the whole] creation [all nature] waits eagerly for the children of God to be revealed."*
> – Romans 8:19 AMP

What are they waiting for? **They are waiting for you** —believers filled with the power of God—to manifest the solutions the world so desperately needs. The world is in chaos, and its systems are failing. Political, economic, and social structures are crumbling, and humanity is searching for answers.

Think about Esther in the Bible. She did not sit back and watch her people perish in despair. She became the solution in a time of national crisis. Her obedience and courage saved the entire Jewish people from extinction.

> *"For if you remain silent at this time, liberation and rescue will arise for the Jews from another place, and you and your father's house will perish [since you did not help when you had the chance]. And who knows whether you have attained royalty for such a time as this [and for this very purpose]?"*
> – Esther 4:14 AMP

In the same way, you are called to rise to the occasion, step into positions of influence, and offer divine solutions to the problems that surround you. **But to become the solution, you must walk in fullness.** You cannot offer what you do not have, and you cannot distribute what you have not first received. Let us explore understanding how to step into the fullness of your Kingdom authority so that you can be a fruitful distributor of God's glory.

WHAT DOES IT MEAN TO WALK IN FULLNESS?

Walking in fullness means that you are living in the complete understanding of who you are in Christ and what He has made available to you. It is not enough to know that God has called you to great things; you must operate from the place of fullness, knowing that **everything you need has already been provided for by God.**

> *"Every spiritual blessing in the heavenly realm has already been lavished upon us as a love gift from our wonderful heavenly Father, the Father of our Lord Jesus."*
>
> – Ephesians 1:3 TPT

You have the resources of heaven at your disposal, and **the only thing that limits you is your understanding of what you have access to.** God has blessed us in the heavenly realms with every spiritual blessing in Christ. This means you are not lacking in any area—whether it is in the area of wisdom, power, provision, or courage.

To walk in fullness means to live in the complete and abundant life that God has designed for you. Fullness refers to a state of being where you are completely filled and satisfied —spiritually, emotionally, mentally, and physically. It is living with a **deep sense of purpose,** knowing that you lack nothing because God's presence, provision, and power are operating fully in your life.

Walking in fullness means embracing the promises of God without limits, not just surviving or scraping by, but living in the overflow of His grace and blessings. Fullness is experiencing the abundant life that Jesus spoke of in John 10:10, where He said, *"I have come that they may have life, and have it to the full."*

It also involves the totality of Christ's presence in your life—having your needs met and being empowered to meet the needs of others. It's about living a life that reflects God's glory, love, and provision, being spiritually enriched so that you can pour out to others, manifesting His Kingdom in every area of life.

In essence, **walking in fullness is not just about receiving;** it is about operating from a place of wholeness and abundance that equips you to be a blessing to others and distribute the fullness you have received from God. It means that you live with an abundance mentality. You no longer see yourself as someone who is in need or lacking, but as someone who already has the solution and is ready to distribute it. You are a conduit through which the power of God flows to bring healing, restoration, and transformation to the world.

BECOMING THE SOLUTION: MOVING FROM SURVIVAL TO DOMINION

Many believers live in survival mode. They pray for God to meet their needs, to get them through the day, or to deliver them from their struggles. While God does meet our needs, this is not the fullness of His plan for your life. **You are meant to move from survival to dominion**.

Consider the story of Joseph. For years, Joseph endured hardship and betrayal. He was thrown into a pit by his brothers, sold into slavery, falsely accused, and imprisoned. But Joseph was not just surviving—he was preparing for dominion. It takes a unique sense of conviction, revelation, and mental shift to rise in the midst of the kind of adversities Joseph faced. Eventually, he rose to a position of power and became the solution to Egypt's famine crisis, not just for the Egyptians, but for the entire region, including his own family *(Genesis 41)*, becoming the chosen one to lead Pharoah's affairs, eventually preserve nations, and pave the way for the generations of Israelites.

Joseph did not spend his life wallowing like a victim and waiting for God to solve his problems. Instead, he allowed God to work in him during his trials, and when the time came, he stepped into his role as a distributor of God's wisdom and provision.

In the same way, you are called to be the solution to the world's famine—whether that famine is spiritual, emotional, financial, mental, or relational. You are not just waiting for a miracle; **you are the miracle the world is waiting for.**

Practical Steps to Becoming a Solution

To walk in the fullness of God and become the solution to the world's problems, there are several practical steps you can take:

1. **Develop a Strong Prayer Life:**

   Prayer is the foundation of your authority. Through prayer, you align yourself with God's will and receive divine strategies. As you grow in prayer, God will reveal to you the specific solutions you are called to bring into your sphere of influence.

2. **Consider Daniel in the Bible:**

   In Daniel 10:12, we see that Daniel's prayers stirred the heavens.

   > *"He reassured me by saying, "Daniel, don't be afraid, for I have come to bring to you the answer to your prayer. From the first day you sought to understand the revelation and humbled yourself before God, your words were heard in heaven."*
   > – Daniel 10:12 TPT

   Even when the enemy sought to block the answer, Daniel's persistent prayer released the angelic assistance that was needed. Persistent prayer breaks barriers and releases divine answers.

3. **Embrace Your Unique Calling:**

   Not everyone is called to the same thing. God has uniquely equipped you to be a solution in a particular area. Some are called to be financial distributors, others to bring healing, and others to release wisdom. When you know your calling, you can focus on the area where

God has empowered you to be a solution.

"....And who knows whether you have attained royalty for such a time as this [and for this very purpose]?"
                                        – Esther 4:14 AMP

Esther embraced her calling when she recognized that she was placed in the palace for such a time as this. She did not shy away from the responsibility but stepped into it fully, knowing that her obedience would lead to the salvation of her people.

4. **Release What Is in Your Hand:**

   Just as the widow at Zarephath gave Elijah the little oil she had and God multiplied it *(1 Kings 17:8-16)*, you must be willing to release what is in your hand. Often, the solution to someone else's problem is already within your reach, but it requires faith to release it. When you give—whether it's time, resources, or spiritual gifts—God multiplies it and uses it to bring solutions to those around you.

5. **Collaborate with Others:**

   Walking in fullness does not mean walking alone. In fact, God often brings people into your life to help you manifest His solutions. This is the power of synergy. When believers unite, they amplify their impact. The church, when operating as one body, is a powerful force of solutions.

In Acts 2, we see the early church walking in unity and power, and as a result, they became the solution to their community's needs. They met the needs of the poor, healed the sick, and shared the gospel with boldness. Their unity and collaboration made them unstoppable.

BECOMING A SOLUTION IN YOUR COMMUNITY

Let me tell you the story of a young woman named Grace. She had a burden for the children in her neighborhood who had no access to education. For months, she prayed, asking God to send someone to help. Then one day, God showed her that she was the solution. With nothing more than a few books and a heart for the children, she started a small school in her backyard. Soon, word spread, and more children came.

As Grace released what she had, God multiplied it. Donations came in, volunteers joined her, and today, that backyard school has grown into a fully-fledged educational center that is transforming the lives of hundreds of children. Grace became the solution because she was willing to walk in fullness and release what God had placed in her hands.

The world is not waiting for more political leaders, economic reform, or technological advancements. These things have their place, but they cannot solve the deeper problems that plague humanity. **The world is waiting for the sons and daughters of God to step into their fullness and release the solutions that only come from heaven.**

God has given you everything you need to be a distributor of His solutions. You carry the answers to the problems in your family, workplace, community, and nation. Do not wait for someone else to step up. You are called to rise and take your place as a solution-bearer in this generation.

Walking in fullness is not about achieving perfection or never experiencing challenges. It is about living from the place of divine abundance, knowing that God has equipped you to be the solution wherever you go. You are not a victim of circumstances, waiting for someone else to solve your problems. You are a child of God, filled with His Spirit, and you have been given the authority and power to bring His Kingdom solutions to a broken world.

As you step into your role as a distributor, remember that creation is waiting. The world is eagerly anticipating the manifestation of the sons and daughters of God. Will you answer the call and walk in the fullness of your Kingdom authority? Will you rise to become the solution that God has destined you to be?

CHAPTER 8

LIVING AS A KINGDOM DISTRIBUTOR: THE JOURNEY OF IMPACT

"For the one who has will be given more, until he overflows with abundance. And the one with hardly anything, even what little he has will be taken from him."

– Matthew 25:29 TPT

As we approach the closing of this journey from consumer to distributor, it is essential to understand that living as a Kingdom distributor is not a one-time event or a temporary experience; it is a lifestyle—a continuous journey of impact, purpose, and fulfillment. In this chapter, we explore what it means to live out this calling daily, bringing it into the practical realities of life, and becoming vessels through which God's Kingdom flows and impacts the world.

THE RESPONSIBILITY OF STEWARDSHIP

To live as a Kingdom distributor is to live as a steward of the gifts, resources, and blessings that God has entrusted to you.

"Take the thousand and give it to the one who risked the most. And get rid of this "play-it-safe" who won't go out on a limb. Throw him out into utter darkness."
– Matthew 25:29 MSG

This reminds us of the importance of multiplying what we have been given. The parable of the talents is a powerful illustration of this principle. Each servant was given a portion according to their ability, and those who multiplied their talents were rewarded with more. But the one who buried his talent out of fear or negligence lost even what he had.

Being a **Kingdom distributor** means you understand the responsibility that comes with God's blessings. The gifts, resources, influence, and authority you have been given are not for personal consumption alone; they are tools for Kingdom expansion. You are called to multiply what you have received by pouring it into others, growing the impact of God's work through you.

With great abundance comes great responsibility. God expects you to steward the overflow He entrusts to you wisely. This does not mean holding back or hoarding what you have received but being faithful in managing the resources, gifts, and opportunities God has given you.

"Those who live to bless others will have blessings heaped upon them, and the one who pours out his life to pour out blessings will be saturated with favor."
– Proverbs 11:25 TPT

As you refresh others, God refreshes you. The key to continual overflow is to keep releasing what you've been given. Stewardship is not about guarding what you have —it is about multiplying it through generosity and wise distribution.

THE POWER OF INFLUENCE

Influence in the modern world is sometimes understood via the prism of social media following, financial riches, or celebrity reputation. Many people define success in our era by their capacity to draw attention or their financial situation. Influence, in the Kingdom of God, is not about appearances or worldly success, though. Walking in Christ's authority and applying that influence to bring about good change for the life of others is what defines true impact. It's about how you treat and inspire people around you, not only about your platform or large following. You have impact as a Kingdom distributor outside of a pulpit or stage. It goes much beyond—to your family, your workplace, your neighborhood, and even the little everyday exchanges you engage in.

Consider Joseph found in the Bible. Joseph, sold into slavery by his own brothers, had every cause to feel helpless and develop a defeated attitude. He might have gotten resentful, concentrated on what he lacked, and let his circumstances control his behavior. But Joseph realized that his actual power came from God's direction for his life. Joseph embraced his responsibilities and walked in his power first in Potiphar's house, then in prison, and lastly as a king in Egypt even in the middle of suffering. His impact went beyond his surroundings; it included countries since he started distributing answers during a worldwide famine. Joseph saved many lives since he complemented God's will.

In the Kingdom of God, influence is a quite strong power. It's about the difference you influence in the life around you, not about your name's popularity or count of recognition. When in line with God's will, influence becomes an instrument for spreading His Kingdom and changing lives. No matter where they live, every believer is expected to be a person of influence. Placed here to radiate His truth and love in all spheres of the planet, we are the salt of the earth and the light of the globe as Jesus Himself declared (Matthew 5:13–14).

> *"Your lives are like salt among the people. But if you, like salt, become bland, how can your 'saltiness' be restored? Flavorless salt is good for nothing and will be thrown out and trampled on by others."*
> – Matthew 5:13-14 TPT

Salt preserves, and light illuminates—both are agents of change. In the same way, your life is meant to preserve and transform the world around you, bringing the influence of God's Kingdom into every sphere you touch.

In the same way, God is calling you to step into your sphere of influence as a distributor. Whether you are a teacher, business owner, parent, or leader, you have a unique role to play in God's Kingdom. Your influence, when submitted to God, can transform lives, communities, and even generations.

WALKING IN ABUNDANCE, NOT SCARCITY

One of the biggest hindrances to living as a Kingdom distributor is a scarcity mentality. This mindset says, "I do not have enough" or "If I give, I will run out." But God's Kingdom operates on the principle of abundance.

> *"Give generously, and generous gifts will be given back to you, shaken down to make room for more. Abundant gifts will pour out upon you with such an overflowing measure that it will run over the top!"*
> – Luke 6:38 TPT

The world operates in fear of running out, but as a Kingdom distributor, you must embrace the mindset that God's resources are limitless. The more you release what you have—whether it is time, finances, love, or wisdom—the more God will supply you with greater measures. Think of it as tapping into a divine supply chain that never runs dry. When you give, you make room for more, and God ensures that you are always walking in overflow.

A robust biblical example of this principle can be seen in the story of the widow of Zarephath *(1 Kings 17:8-16)*. During a time of severe famine, the widow was preparing her last meal for herself and her son, expecting to die soon after. But when the prophet Elijah asked her to make a small loaf of bread for him first, she stepped out in faith, releasing the little she had. Her act of obedience and faith triggered a miracle —her oil and flour did not run out throughout the famine. This story illustrates that when we give, **even from what seems like a small or insufficient supply, God multiplies it.** The widow moved from a consumer mindset (focusing on her lack) to a distributor mindset (giving to Elijah), and her obedience led to supernatural provision.

KINGDOM DISTRIBUTION IN ACTION

Living as a Kingdom distributor is not just a concept; it requires intentionality and practical application. Here are several steps you can take to live out this calling:

1. **Identify Your Resources:**

   Take stock of the gifts, talents, influence, and resources God has placed in your hands. You may not have everything, but you have something to contribute.

2. **Stay Connected to the Source:**

   Like the widow's jar of oil, your supply is sustained by staying connected to God. Make prayer, worship, and time in the Word a daily habit, allowing God to refill and refresh you continually.

3. **Invest in Others:**

Seek opportunities to pour into others—whether it is mentoring someone, serving in your church, or contributing financially to Kingdom causes. Look beyond your needs and focus on being a blessing.

4. Be Bold in Faith:

Do not hesitate to step out and give, even when it stretches you. God is faithful in supplying every need according to His riches in glory.

"And my God will liberally supply (fill until full) your every need according to His riches in glory in Christ Jesus."
— Philippians 4:19 AMP

5. Watch for the Harvest:

As a farmer expects a crop after planting seeds, expect God to multiply what you have sown. Whether peace, joy, provision, or opportunities, God's harvest is always more significant than the seed you plant.

BECOMING THE SOLUTION: THE ESTHER MANDATE

The story of Esther features one of the most important pictures of what it means to live life distributing the Kingdom. Since Esther was raised to be queen in the Persian monarchy, she possessed a great degree of power and privilege. She still had to decide whether to say nothing while her people, the Jews, were under enormous risk from an order meant to wipe them off. Esther knew that her position of power came with responsibility, hence even if she could protect her personal well-being and avoid taking any risks, this was inevitable. Esther decided to embrace her divine position as a deliverer of deliverance instead of choosing her own personal comfort. To demand that her people be safeguarded, she bravely moved, risking her life, and went to the king without an invitation. The saving grace for a whole country was her courage to act in front of danger.

Esther's story teaches us a crucial lesson: our kingdom's distribution often reflects the needs of other people rather powerfully. It is about being there for others when they need help instead of concentrating on ourselves; it is not only about achieving personal achievement or comfort for ourselves. God places us in circumstances whereby we may provide answers for the issues arising in our surroundings. Every crisis, famine, or spiritual drought his people are elevated to be a source of hope and deliverance. This is valid in all kinds of situation. Like Esther, we are called to be the response to another person's need and to behave selflessly in line with God's will for us.

In the same line, God has positioned you in an unparalleled state at this moment. People all around are yearning for solutions, especially Kingdom distributors who will show compassion, courage, and faith. Your impact as you answer this call will not only affect the individuals in your close circle but also leave a legacy for grandchildren and children to inherit.

THE JOURNEY OF CONTINUAL GROWTH & A LIFE OF ETERNAL IMPACT

Living as a Kingdom distributor is a lifelong journey of growth. There will be seasons of stretching, sacrifice, and challenges, but each step brings you closer to fulfilling
God's purpose for your life. As you continue to walk in this calling, God will enlarge your capacity to give, bless, and impact others. You will experience the joy of living in overflow—for yourself and everyone around you.

Living as a Kingdom distributor is about walking in fullness, faith, and favor. It is about moving from a mindset of lack to a life of abundant giving. The more you release, the more you will receive, and the more you receive, the greater your capacity to distribute God's glory, grace, and power to the world.

As a Kingdom distributor, your influence is eternal. The seeds you plant, the lives you touch, and the impact you make will bear fruit long after you are gone. When you walk in obedience to God and use your influence to reflect His glory, you become a vessel of transformation, both now and for generations to come.

Remember, the world is not waiting for more consumers but for distributors. The time is now for you to rise and become the solution God has destined you to be. As you walk in this calling, you will not only transform your life but leave a legacy of impact that will echo into eternity.

CONCLUSION

I gnorance is one of the most dangerous positions you can find yourself in as a believer, not because God's promises aren't true or His power isn't real, but because ignorance robs you of the ability to access the full scope of what He has already provided. I tell you the truth, it is tragic to see that many Christians live their lives struggling, defeated, and overwhelmed simply because they do not know the authority that God has granted them or how to unleash it. Hosea 4:6 says "My people are destroyed for lack of knowledge," and this lack of understanding leads to a life of frustration where you are constantly begging for what God has already placed in your hands.

When Jesus declared in Matthew 28:18, "All authority in heaven and on earth has been given to me," He wasn't just making a statement about His own victory; He was actually extending that authority to all who believe in Him. Yet, so many believers fail to walk in this authority because they do not realize it is theirs; they live as though they are powerless, constantly fighting battles that have already been won, and pleading for blessings that have already been given. Think about it, how often do you pray prayers that are filled with fear and uncertainty, asking God to do things He has already empowered you to do? For example, when you face spiritual attacks, you may cry out for God to intervene, forgetting that Luke 10:19 says, "I have given you authority to trample on snakes and scorpions and to overcome all the power of the enemy; nothing will harm you." The authority to resist the enemy, to command situations to change, and to enforce the will of God on earth is already yours. Yet, if you don't know this, you will live like a victim, constantly reacting to life's challenges instead of standing in the victory Christ has secured for you.

The cost of ignorance is far greater than most people realize because it doesn't just affect your spiritual life; it eats deep into every area of your existence. But I thank God that you have now read this book and your eyes have been opened to the authority that God has given. It's time for you to go forth and continually enforce that authority to see victory in every aspect of your life. The enemy uses ignorance as a weapon because he knows that an uninformed believer is a powerless believer, but thank God that now you are no more ignorant.

Are you set to take kingdoms, and nations and to subdue anything that the kingdom of God has not ordained in your life? The its time to take action because it's those who do the word that are blessed and not just those who know it.

It's time for you to go forth and unleash your kingdom authority! God is with you!

SALVATION PAGE

Dear Beloved,

God loves you deeply, and He has brought you to this moment for a reason. No matter your past, His love and forgiveness are available to you right now.

The Bible says in John 3:16, "For God so loved the world that He gave His one and only Son, that whoever believes in Him shall not perish but have eternal life." Jesus Christ came to save you, offering a new life filled with purpose and peace.

If you're ready to accept Jesus as your Lord and Savior, pray this simple prayer:

The Salvation Prayer

"Heavenly Father, I come to You in the Name of Jesus. I acknowledge that I am a sinner in need of a Savior. I believe that Jesus Christ is Your Son, that He died for my sins, and that You raised Him from the dead. I repent of my sins and turn to You with my whole heart. Jesus, I ask You to come into my life. Be my Lord and my Savior. I surrender my life to You. Fill me with Your Holy Spirit, guide me on the path of righteousness, and help me to follow Your script for my life. Thank you, Father, for saving me. In the name of Jesus. Amen."

Welcome to the Family of God!

If you have just prayed this prayer, Congratulations! You are now a child of God, and heaven is rejoicing. Your journey has begun, and we're here to support you as you grow in faith and discover God's amazing plans for you.

www.ingramcontent.com/pod-product-compliance
Lightning Source LLC
Chambersburg PA
CBHW071905020426
42331CB00010B/2671